# Inside the

# EGYPTIAN
# MUSEUM

# with ZAHI HAWASS

**Photographs**
**SANDRO VANNINI**

HERITAGE
WORLD PRESS

Inside the
# EGYPTIAN MUSEUM
## with ZAHI HAWASS

**Photographs by**
**SANDRO VANNINI**

**Heritage World Press Ltd**
Reg Number: 6965934
337 Bath Road
Slough
Berkshire SL1 5PR
United Kingdom

*www.heritageworldpress.com*

First published in the United Kingdom in 2009 by Heritage World Press

**Produced by**
 Laboratoriorosso srl - Viterbo, Italy

**Production Project Manager**
Luca Vannini

**Edited by**
Garry Shaw

**Photography postproduction**
Massimo Luciani

**Graphic Design**
 Silvia Cruciani - Studio Frasi

A CIP catalogue record of this book is available from the British Library

ISBN: 978-1-907397-00-4

Printed and bound in the People's Republic of China through DfM Ltd

# Acknowledgements

*Many people have helped me to complete this book. First I would like to thank the great photographer Sandro Vannini who took the wonderful photos, and also encouraged me to write the script. Also I would like to thank the members of my scientific office at the SCA, who helped me to collect some of the published data. Finally, a very special thanks goes to Garry Shaw, who worked very hard to edit this book. To all I give my thanks.*

*The work in the Cairo Museum has taken a long, long time, and a lot of people have been involved. Firstly, I would like to acknowledge Dr Wafaa el Saddik, Director of the Egyptian Museum in Cairo, as she has been a wonderful host for my team and myself, and her treasured assistant Albert Girgis Ghaly, who helped me to manage all our bureaucratic needs. Then I would like to acknowledge all the curators of the different sections for their patience whilst waiting many long hours for my work. For the same reason I would like to acknowledge the people responsible for security. All this work is a team project and would be impossible without the people working with me in Cairo and in Italy: Mohamed Megahed, my tireless Egyptology advisor and the staff in the Cairo Museum, Ramadan Elsayed Abdelmotelb, Ramadan Hamed Khalaf, Abdallah Hassan Helmy and Mounir Lotfy Abdalliem. In my office in Viterbo, where the digital work was carried out, I would like to acknowledge Massimo Luciani, responsible for the digital elaboration of all the images, my son Luca, Project Manager, and my wife Maria Rita, the main coordinator of all our work. Last but (certainly) not least, many thanks to Zahi Hawass, who passed to me his everlasting love for Archaeology.*

# Inside the **Egyptian Museum**
## with ZAHI HAWASS

## Contents

# I
# Introduction

# Introduction

The architect of the Egyptian Museum, Marcel Dourgnon, was a genius. He understood the cultural and chronological divisions of Egyptian civilisation; notably, how it is divided into four major phases, each distinct from one another. As every foreigner who comes to Egypt, Dourgnon became Egyptianised, and so designed the exterior of the Egyptian Museum to reflect the Pharaonic, Greco-Roman, Coptic and Islamic phases of Egyptian history. In imitation of the ancient temples, the architect crafted the museum's entrance as a Pharaonic period pylon - a square façade with large gates; above the exterior doorways are Greek inscriptions and Greco-Roman style statues; the two pillars flanking the entrance, as well as the cornice above them, were inspired by Coptic art and the European traditions of Christianity; finally, the large dome attached to the roof, 34 metres in height, was made in the Islamic style. Thus, the architecture of the Egyptian Museum is a creative work of art in itself, reflecting the long history of Egypt.

The history of the Egyptian Museum began in 1830 when Mohammed Ali Pasha received a letter from Jean-François Champollion, the French scholar who discovered the key to ancient Egyptian hieroglyphs, requesting that a building for the protection of Egyptian monuments be constructed. The Pasha approved his request and, on August 5th 1835, decreed that all Pharaonic period objects be collected and sent to Sheikh Refaa el-Tahtawy, director of a language school in Ezbekieh, and to Yossef Diger Effendi, an Egyptian intellectual in charge of the inspection of Upper Egyptian archaeological sites. In 1848, the collection amassed was placed in a storage room owned by the language school. The Egyptian government then appointed Linant de Bellefonds to review the objects. Unfortunately, over time, many of the artefacts were stolen and so in 1851, under Abbas I, the collection was moved to a room at the Citadel that was inaccessible to the public. Then, in 1855, much of the collection was offered to Archduke Maximilian of Austria as a gift and was incorporated into the collection of the Museum of Art History in Vienna. On June 1st, 1858, Khedive Said Pasha appointed Auguste Mariette as the Head of the Antiquities Service. Mariette had acquired much needed experience while working at the

Louvre between 1855 and 1861, experience that was crucial when establishing the new Egyptian Museum. According to a letter he wrote to Henri Brugsch on April 10th 1859, his plan was to build the new museum at Giza, around the Valley Temple of Khafre (which he had discovered in 1854). He began assembling the artefacts from his excavations inside four rooms at the Nile Navigation Company building at Bulaq harbour. As time progressed and further discoveries were made all over Egypt, Mariette was compelled to add new rooms to the original building. In October 1863, Khedive Ismail Pasha officially opened the Bulaq Museum to the public. Its masterpiece was a statue of the Divine Wife Amunerdis, discovered in the Temple of Montu at Karnak in 1858 (and which can still be seen in the Egyptian Museum in Tahrir Square today). The Bulaq Museum also had the treasure of Iakhhotep on display, which was found at Dra Abu el-Naga on the West Bank of the Nile at Luxor, as well as other major discoveries unearthed by foreign archaeological teams.

Having been built on the banks of the Nile, the Bulaq Museum was always in danger of flooding. In 1878, one of the worst floods in years hit and destroyed much of the building. Mariette restored the damaged areas but quickly realised that this location was no longer suitable to house the priceless ancient relics; not only were the objects in constant danger of water damage, but the museum no longer had enough room to house the new artefacts that were constantly being found by the increasing number of excavation teams.

In January 1881, just a few days before the death of Mariette, French archaeologist Gaston Maspero arrived in Egypt and, by February, was appointed Director of the Antiquities Service and head of the Bulaq Museum. As of November 1881, Maspero requested further renovations at the Museum in continuation of Mariette's work. He also continued to study the antiquities in the museum and arranged the exhibits in the halls for the next five years. The details of his work were recorded for prosperity through the official documents and personal letters sent to his wife, Louisa, now kept in the Egyptian archives. In his letters, Maspero would recount in detail any and all his efforts concerning the artefacts and his scientific publications. One of his greatest achievements was the publication of the Complete Guide to the Bulaq Museum in 1883.

Victor Loret, a member of the French Expedition and student of Maspero, met up with his professor in Egypt. On January 15th 1881, Loret toured the Bulaq Museum for the first time; he wrote about this visit in his diaries, found at Milan University in 2002. Loret described the halls of the museum, noted the location of the objects, took photos of the building and drew its plan. He also created a filing system, made line drawings of the artefacts and traced their inscriptions. He performed the duties of a curator. All this information was found hidden inside the pages of Loret's diaries; their discovery has helped retrace the journey of the various artefacts in the Bulaq Museum collection in 1881.

A man named Ahmed Pasha Kamal, the first Egyptian archaeologist, was brought in to assist Maspero as a translator. During his second year working for Maspero, he opened a School of Archaeology at the Bulaq Museum, where many important students learnt their skills. They include such names as Mohammed Shaban and Hassan Hosni, who went on to become Inspector of Antiquities and then Assistant Curator at the Giza Museum, and who published numerous object catalogues and archaeological works in Arabic. It was also around this time that Maspero and Ahmed Pasha Kamal began pressuring the local authorities to build small local museums within the various Egyptian governorates.

Ahmed Pasha Kamal would later go on to work with Emile Brugsch on important archaeological missions, such as the clearance of the mummy cachette at Deir el-Bahari in 1881. The Abdel Rassul family first discovered this famous cachette in 1871, and kept its existence and location quiet for ten years. Eventually, Maspero stumbled upon their secret. He sent Ahmed Pasha Kamal with Brugsch to Luxor and, with the help of the police in Qurna, they located the entrance to the Deir el-Bahari cachette. This story has been retold in many books and articles, as well as in an Egyptian film called *The Night of Counting the Years* (also known as *The Mummy*), by the director Shadi Abdel Salam.

It was finally decided that the location of the Bulaq Museum was not safe for the artefacts. Therefore, in 1887, the Egyptian government moved the collection temporarily to the Palace of Ismail Pasha at Giza (also known as the Giza Museum); this palace is now the location of the Giza Zoo. On January 12th 1890, the Khedive Tawfiq opened forty-five halls of the Giza Museum to the public. He then moved the tomb of Mariette from Bulaq to the new Giza Museum. Finally, in 1891, the Khedive Tawfiq opened the remaining forty-six halls of the palace.

Victor Loret had an office in the new museum at Giza. Loret, who would be Director of Egyptian Antiquities from November 1897 to the end of 1899, invested much of his time and effort into this museum, so much so that he hardly ever left it. He would only ever leave to perform inspections or to go on excavation at Saqqara or in the Valley of the Kings. One of Loret's most important discoveries was the tomb of Amenhotep II, which he found in 1898 almost intact. Behind a decorated wall in the tomb was a cachette of twelve mummies. Loret left the mummies inside the cachette, but they were later moved to the Egyptian Museum by Howard Carter. Some of the mummies that Carter left behind in the tomb, such as the 'Elder Lady' and the 'Younger Lady,' have recently been studied as part of our search for the family of King Tutankhamun. Our findings have turned out to be crucial in the reconstruction and understanding of Egypt's past.

The Giza Museum did not remain open for very long. The British Egyptologist Sir E. A. Wallis Budge wrote that the royal mummies seemed sad because they were kept in an unsuitable place. The halls were painted blue, gold and orange, and the ceiling was decorated with drawings of Cupid and Venus. Although quite beautiful, the surroundings were not suitable to display the great Pharaohs of Egypt. Moreover, it was thought that the Giza Museum was not secure enough to house the great discoveries being brought to light almost every day. Therefore, Jacques de Morgan, Director of the Antiquities Service from 1892 to 1897, renewed the pressure on the Egyptian government to construct a new museum.

Between 1893 and 1895, an international competition was launched seeking an architect to build the new Egyptian Museum. This was a very impressive decision for its time. Choosing an architect internationally demonstrated that the Egyptian monuments were not restricted to the people of Egypt, but that they belonged to the entire world. It was decided that the new museum would be built in the heart of Cairo, near the British army barracks, now Tahrir Square. The committee received eighty-seven architectural proposals, including designs that took the form of pyramids. In the end, they chose the proposal of Marcel Dourgnon, creating the museum that we have today.

An Italian company, called Garozzo-Zaffarani, was contracted between 1897 and 1901 to build the museum. The stone foundation was laid on April 1st 1897 in the presence of Khedive Abbas Helmi II, Jacques de Morgan, Director of Egyptian Antiquities, and the architect, Marcel Dourgnon. Once construction was completed, Maspero and his assistant, Alessandro Barsanti, had the difficult task of moving five thousand boxes of Egyptian artefacts from the Giza Museum, as well as from other storage areas, to the new museum. This would prove to be the most difficult endeavour of the time. The Egyptian Museum officially opened to the public on November 15th 1902. The remains of Auguste Mariette were moved to the museum's garden and a shrine was erected in his honour. Today, statues of foreign and Egyptian archaeologists surround him.

In 2002, when I was appointed Head of the Antiquities Service, I gave the Egyptian Museum my full attention. It is one of the most important museums in the world and contains the largest collection of Pharaonic artefacts anywhere. I also learned that it is one of the few museums in the world purposely built to house and protect antiquities; other museums had simply been converted from large villas.

The museum's centennial was fast approaching, and I began to prepare for its celebration; the outside walls of the museum were given a fresh coat of paint and part of the basement was converted into an exhibition hall specifically for the centennial. The event was spectacular; a large tent was erected west of the building and songs were sung in the garden. Mrs. Mubarak, the Egyptian First Lady, and Farouk Hosni, Minister of Culture, opened the festivities. A twenty-minute National Geographic documentary was shown inside the tent, followed by speeches honouring the workers of the museum, down to the guards and manual workers. A new postage stamp and a medal commemorating the museum's centennial were issued. It is a day that I will never forget.

For the past few years, I have been working to bring the Egyptian Museum into the 21st century and into the hearts and minds of people from around the world. My efforts, however, have also been turned towards the development of other museums around Egypt. In the shadow of the pyramids at Giza, we are working on the construction of the new Grand Egyptian Museum. As with the Egyptian Museum in Tahrir, an international competition was launched to find the perfect architectural proposal. We aim to open the Grand Egyptian Museum in 2014; it will house such Egyptian art collections as the funerary equipment of Queen Hetepheres, the gold of Tanis and the treasures of Tutankhamun, including the famous golden mask. We are also planning to relocate the two solar boats of Khufu there – one is currently in the Boat Museum at Giza, while the second one still lies within its boat pit and is being restored by a Japanese team. In 2006, the colossal statue of Ramesses II was moved from Ramesses Square in front of Cairo railway station, to the new museum. Here, it will become the centrepiece of the Great Hall known as the Gallery of Kings. In total, about 40% of the artefacts from the Egyptian Museum will be moved there.

The Grand Egyptian Museum will be one of the largest museums in the world, exhibiting over 5,000 artefacts. We are sparing no expense, implementing the latest technology and new collections management systems in order to aid scholars in their research. The construction of state-of-the-art restoration and conservation laboratories has already been completed and we have also finished building secure halls and magazines with enough room to store over 150,000 objects. Our philosophy at the museum is to display the collections in the most enjoyable and appealing way, while also focusing on culture and education. Objects from all Pharaonic periods, from the Predynastic to the Late Period, will be on display, while the use of the latest technology will connect it to museums all over the world. The Grand Egyptian Museum will stand out as a symbol of the new millennium through the use of modern designs in architecture, the incorporation of an IMAX theatre and in the innovative educational methods used to present ancient Egyptian civilisation, specifically its daily life and art. The selection committee received over 2,000 architectural proposals, each with its own vision. In the end, we chose a project presented by a Chinese architect living in Dublin.

The National Museum of Egyptian Civilisation will also be completed soon in Fustat near Old Cairo. About 20% of the objects in the Egyptian Museum will be moved there. The location is amazing; the museum looks out over a lake, while in the distance, the visitor can see Coptic Cairo, Islamic Cairo and some monuments dating to the Pharaonic Period. The museum will display the history of Egypt, from prehistoric times to the era of Mohammed Ali, with such topics as agriculture, industry, kingship and social life being presented. A few select objects will be moved from the Egyptian Museum to the National Museum of Egyptian Civilisation upon its completion.

The idea for a National Museum began as early as 1978 when the Supreme Council of Antiquities decided to build the Nubian Museum in Aswan in order to house the monuments saved from the Nubian temples that had been flooded after the construction of the Aswan High Dam. Originally the decision was taken to locate the National Museum near the Cairo Opera House in Zamalek but a committee voted to erect it in Fustat, in Old Cairo. An architectural competition was held in 1984 and was won by an Egyptian architect. In 2000, a survey of the site was conducted, then, in 2002, the First Lady of Egypt, Mrs. Mubarak, officially laid the first brick in the museum's foundation. UNESCO has been continuously working with us with regard to the National Museum, offering technical assistance and support. The museum will be the size of twenty-two fedans. It will contain a reception area, shops, cafes, restaurants, a theatre, restoration laboratories, administrative offices, and storage magazines, as well as the main focal point of the building - the exhibition halls.

Upon visiting the National Museum of Egyptian Civilisation, the visitor will travel in time to Egypt's Predynastic Period. He will wander through the ages, entering the Pharaonic Period, the Greco-Roman Period, the Coptic Period, the Islamic Period and then exit in the modern age. The second section of the museum focuses on specific topics, such as the dawn of civilisation, daily life, agriculture and the miracle of the Nile. The land of Egypt is surrounded by desert, making the Nile crucial for the survival of the Egyptians. The displays will explain how the Nile was, and is, the backbone of Egyptian society and will demonstrate the methods used in fishing and agriculture. The third section of the museum focuses on writing and science in ancient Egypt; the artefacts and displays here will teach visitors about the various written scripts used in Egypt, the ingenuity of the Egyptian scientists, as well as their understanding of medicine, astronomy, mathematics and mummification. The fourth section relates to architecture, presenting how it developed, as well showing the various types of architectural constructions made by the ancient Egyptians, such as funerary buildings. This exhibit also focuses on ancient Egyptian art; providing examples of sculpture and jewellery, amongst others. The fifth topic presented is Egyptian society; it tells the story of how the Egyptians were the first civilisation in the world to be organised by a centralised government, explains the Egyptian concept of *maat* 'justice' and its role in society and politics, and teaches about the role of women. Finally, the sixth section of the museum deals with religious beliefs - the ancient gods and the afterlife.

The Egyptian Museum in Tahrir Square will not be forgotten. Many new projects have been implemented during my time as Secretary General of the SCA. I have followed their development closely and receive detailed weekly reports on their status from Hisham El-Leithy in my office, whom I appointed to oversee their progress. Currently, as of writing, we are repainting the museum's exterior, so that it returns to the original colour chosen by Dourgnon. It is now shining, like a jewel, in the heart of Cairo and is a light to everyone that sees it. At the eastern side of the museum, a stone wall had been built - this was not part of Dourgnon's original plans for he had intended a tall, iron fence to be erected there. This wall has now been demolished and the area rebuilt in accordance with the original plans. I have also decided to create an open-air museum in this space, including newly restored monuments by the great Egyptian restorer, Lofti Khaled. Recently, we have illuminated the statues and tombs in the museum garden in the hope that, anyone walking by and seeing the beautiful statues in the light, will stop fretting about their problems and feel happy.

We have also effected many changes in the museum basement. This was like a maze and no-one knew the location of any of the objects; most of them were not even registered. First, Sabaah Abdel Razik, a curator in the museum, began to document the artefacts then I hired a company to re-design and modernise the storage areas. We created a small hall for exhibitions on the west side. A section has been converted into offices for the curators, who each now have a beautiful working area with a computer. On the east side we have opened the first DNA laboratory in the world intended purely for the study of mummies. Currently, we are working on designing a children's museum, as well.

In addition, we implemented an important project to create a database of all objects in the museum. Before this project began, the location of many of the artefacts was unknown and more than 70% were not properly documented. I also discovered that many were missing. The American Research Centre in Egypt (ARCE) was keen to help and so appointed Janice Kamrin to oversee the project. She hired many intelligent young people to work with her and has been training them in collections management. I am very proud of their work and I hope that these young people will be the ones who take care of the museum in the future.

Now visitors to the museum will enter through the main entrance - which used to be the entrance and exit - and leave on the western side, through a bookstore. A new, five-star restaurant and cafeteria will also be found here. We are currently in discussions to open the museum until ten o'clock in the evening, so that people will have longer to visit the exhibits each day and it is hoped that these restaurants will encourage people to come at night.

We also intend changing and improving the displays, so that masterpieces will be presented in their archaeological context. For example, the Statue of Khafre, my favourite piece in the museum, will be displayed just as it was found in the king's Valley Temple at Giza. Visitors will be able to view an artefact and understand how it was found, who found it, and see all evidence relating to its discovery. Other rooms will explain the history of Egyptology, allowing visitors to learn about the people who have dedicated their lives to uncovering the mysteries of Egypt's past and whose work has helped fill the museum with these precious artefacts – each an individual insight into an ancient world.

Due to my love of the Egyptian Museum, I thought that it would be wonderful to write a guide to its treasures, and to talk about my favourite objects within. I do hope that you will find it useful and enjoyable.

*Zahi Hawass*
August 2009

# The Ground Floor of the Museum

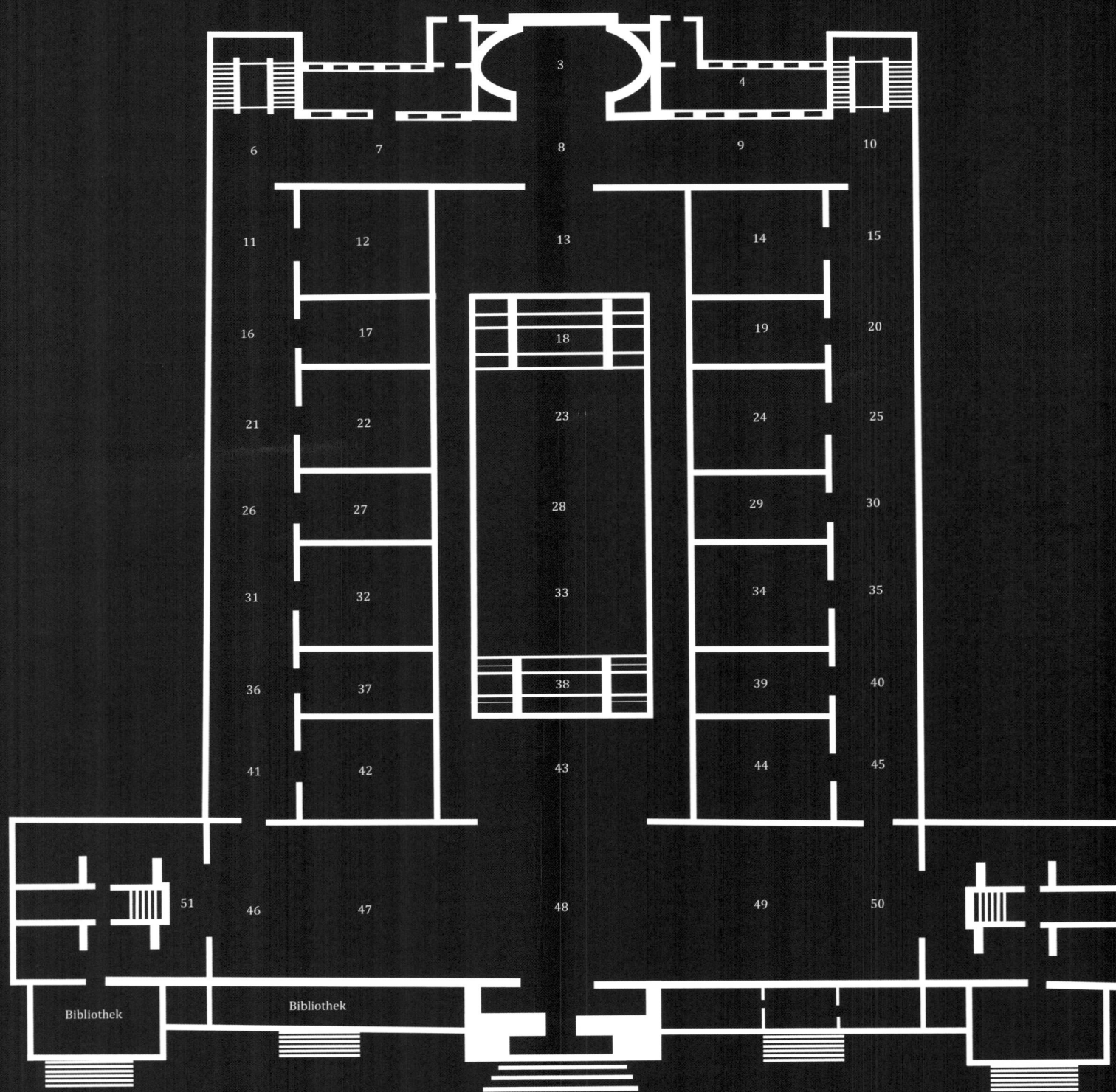

# The Upper Floor
# of the Museum

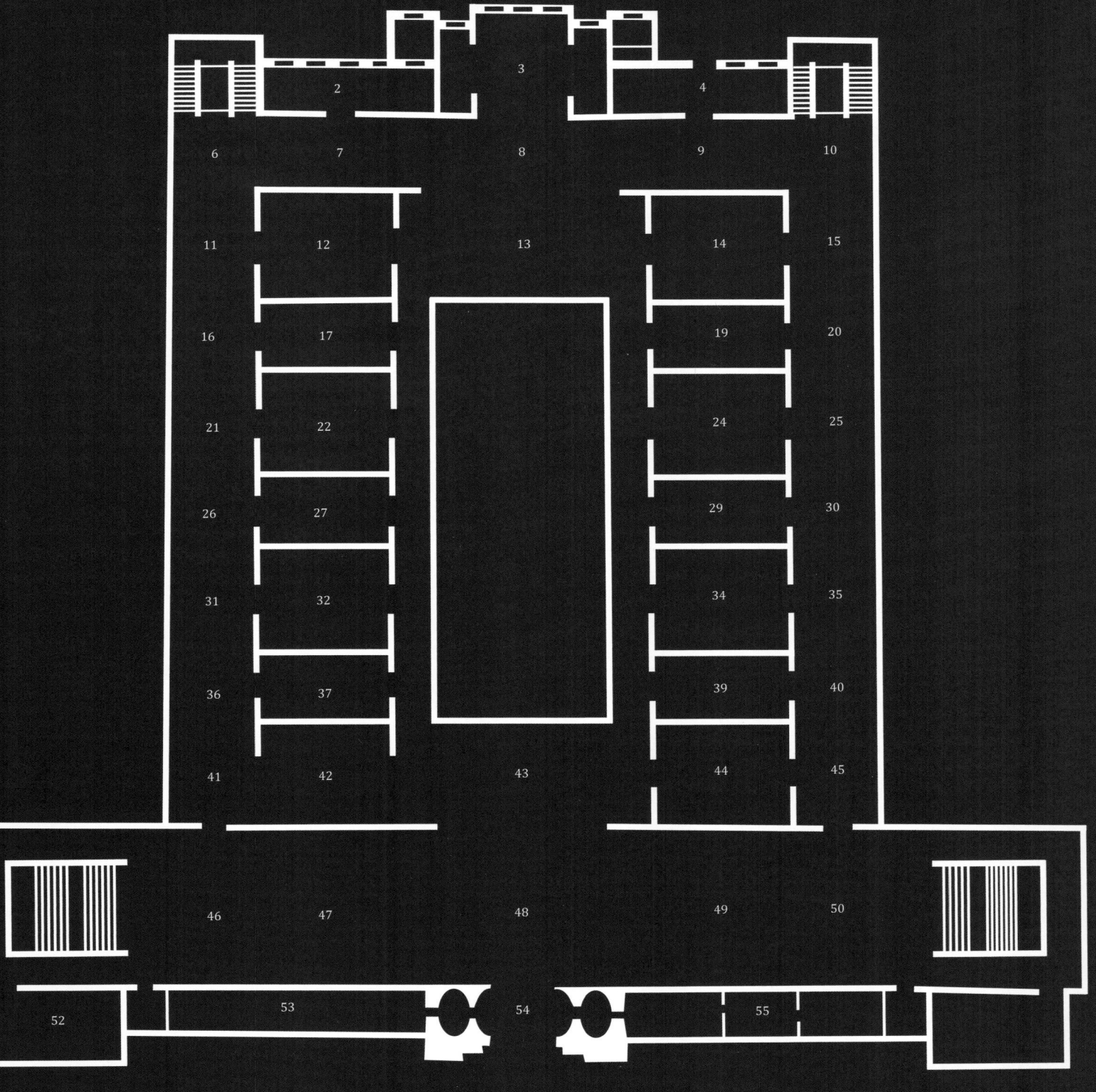

JE 10062

# II
# My Favourite Objects in the Museum

# My Favourite Objects in the Museum

## The Statue of Khafre

*JE 10062; diorite; H. 168cm; 4th Dynasty, Old Kingdom; Khafre's Valley Temple, Giza; Ground Floor, Room 42*

Every Friday, when I go to Tahrir Square to sit in a cafe, I always make sure that I visit the museum for at least half an hour to see my favourite piece – the statue of Khafre. Here, the king can be seen sitting on a lion-legged throne. He wears the nemes-headdress, with a uraeus at the forehead, a false beard and a short kilt. His left arm is placed on his left knee, while his right hand is on his right knee, clasped around a folded cloth – a symbol of authority. On each side of the throne can be seen the sema-tawy motif – representing the unification of Upper and Lower Egypt. I like to walk around this statue and see the hawk on the back of Khafre's head and imagine that it is taking him up to the sky. I also think about the artist who carved the king's face and the muscles of the body; just from the carving, we know that this is the statue of a king. I've walked around this statue hundreds of times and, each time, the world disappears around me and I find myself isolated and alone with it, thinking about this masterpiece of art, created 4,500 years ago. Although the statue looks to be of one person – King Khafre – it is, in fact, a triad. The king is Osiris in death, while the falcon at the back of his head is Horus; the throne upon which the king sits is the hieroglyphic symbol for Isis.

## The Golden Mask of Tutankhamun

*JE 60672; gold, lapis lazuli, quartz, carnelian, turquoise, obsidian, coloured glass; H. 54cm; 18th Dynasty, New Kingdom; Valley of the Kings, Luxor; Upper Floor, Room 3*

This is another masterpiece that has captured my heart. Gazing at the young king's face, I truly believe that there is nothing in the world greater than this mask; it looks so alive. About 11kg in weight and made of gold and semiprecious stones, a beautiful, wide, bejewelled collar adorns his chest and magical inscriptions run around the shoulders and the back. These are taken from Chapter 151b of the Book of the Dead and are meant to help protect the young king. Tutankamun is seen wearing the nemes-headdress, with a uraeus and vulture at his forehead, and his ears are pierced for earrings.

The golden mask was discovered, by Howard Carter, in 1925, covering the head of the

page 20-23 | *The Statue of Khafre* | *JE 10062; diorite; H. 168cm; 4th Dynasty, Old Kingdom; Khafre's Valley Temple, Giza; Ground Floor, Room 42*

JE 10062

23

JE 60672

royal mummy. At the time, he tried to remove it but was unable to – the resins used during the mummification process had acted like a powerful glue sticking the mask to the body. Carter took the mummy outside the tomb and once again tried to remove the mask. Still, he could not and even when he put it under the sun, the resinous glue never weakened. Finally, he took the mummy to the tomb of Seti II and used tools to remove it. In the process, he damaged the mummy completely, breaking it into eighteen pieces.

I saw the current condition of Tutankhamun in 2005, when I went to Luxor to perform a CT scan of the mummy. The moment the mummy was placed in the machine, it stopped working and remained that way for the next hour; for the first time in my life, I began to consider that the curse of Tutankhamun was real. There were many events that day that reinforced my belief in the curse: in the morning, when I left my hotel in Luxor to go to the valley, my driver almost hit and killed a young boy; then, also during my journey, I received a call from my sister who told me that her husband had died. When I arrived at the Valley of the Kings, the assistant to Farouk Hosni, the Minister of Culture, told me that the minister had been taken to hospital. I then gave an interview to a Japanese TV channel and a big storm appeared from nowhere and it began to rain. People all around were saying that the curse of Tutankhamun had returned!

Tutankhamun died at the age of nineteen and there has been much discussion over the years relating to why he died so young. For one, it has been argued that a hole, visible in the back of the king's head, is evidence that Tutankhamun had been murdered. However, during our analysis of the body, we found that this opening had been made during the 18th Dynasty for the insertion of a liquid related to the mummification process. We also discovered that he had a fracture in his left leg and that this may have happened as little as one day before he died. Recently, after our DNA and CT-scan studies, we made two important discoveries: first, Radiologist Ashraf Selim found that Tutankhamun's left leg showed deformities, which may explain why 133 sticks had been placed in the royal tomb. I have analysed some of these sticks, which can be seen on the upper floor of the museum, and found that they had been used during the king's life - the presence of these deformities now explains why such a young man would need so many sticks. There is even a famous scene of the king leaning on a stick in the presence of his wife. The second major discovery was that Tutankhamun suffered from severe malaria and that this was probably the main cause of his death.

Since then, in 2008 – 2009, we have made further discoveries relating to the family of Tutankhamun using CT scans and DNA analyses. We have now identified the mummy of Queen Tiye, whose body had remained in the tomb of Amenhotep II since its discovery, and found that the 'Younger Lady,' also found in the Tomb of Amenhotep II, was the mother of Tutankhamun. We also performed a study on a skeleton found in KV55, in the Valley of the Kings, and found that it is, in fact, the remains of King Akhenaten and that he is the father of Tutankhamun. The elder of the two foetuses, found in the tomb of Tutankhamun, was also given a DNA test, which revealed that it was a daughter of the king. The younger foetus was in too poor a condition to be analysed. Due to our work on the elder foetus, we now hope to be able to identify the mummy of the mother and then, perhaps, also the mummy of Nefertiti.

## The Dwarf Perniankhu

*JE 98944; Basalt; H. 48cm; 4th Dynasty, Old Kingdom; Giza; Ground Floor, Room 42*

I have three babies in the Egyptian Museum: the first is this statue of the dwarf Perniankhu, which you can see on the ground floor of the museum, close to the statue of Khafre. I will never forget the discovery of this statue. When I returned to Egypt from the States in 1987, I wanted to publish the tomb of the Overseer of the Pyramid City of Khufu, Nesutnefer, which is in the western field at Giza. I appointed Mahmoud Afifi to clean the tomb. During our work there, we found at the south side, the wall of another tomb. It was a solid structure, with a serdab (a room in which a statue is normally sealed) attached on the northern side. Inside the serdab, I could see the eyes of this incredible statue - it was so amazing, it looked royal to me - and we began to take down the ceiling of the serdab, in order to gain entry. When I went down into the room and I took the statue in my hand, I had a warm feeling - it was like my baby. It shows the dwarf, Perniankhu, sitting on a low chair, without a back. The dwarf is wearing a traditional, curled wig; his face is strong and displays a quiet serenity, strength and power. His eyes are framed in black and the eyebrows are well-defined. The right hand is placed upon his right thigh and holds the sekhem-sceptre; his left hand, across his chest, holds a long staff. Perniankhu wears a white kilt with a black belt; his legs revealing deformities. His name and titles can be seen in the two vertical lines at the front of the chair; he is described as, 'One who delights his lord every day, the king's dwarf, Perniankhu, of the Great Palace.'

## The Statue of Kai

*JE 99128; limestone; H. 58cm; 5th Dynasty, Old Kingdom; Giza; Ground Floor, Hall 46*

Another one of my favourite pieces in the museum is the statue of Kai, which can also be seen on the Ground Floor. This statue is amazing and I found it in a tomb that I nicknamed the 'Nefertari of Giza,' because of its vibrant colours and beauty. The statue was found behind the southern false door of the tomb and, even before the room had been opened, I could see the statue's crystal eyes gazing back at me. The statue shows Kai sitting on a high-backed chair. He wears a shoulder length wig, decorated with horizontal rows of curls. Each eye is framed in copper, while his eyebrows are in raised relief. The lips are thin and finely drawn. Below, he wears a *wesekh* (broad) collar, composed of seven horizontal bands of blue and green. Tear-shaped pendants hang from the final band of the collar, whilst a counterpoise can be seen at the back. The muscles of the body are well-defined; his right arm is bent across the chest with his hand holding a folded cloth. The left arm is resting on his lap and he sports a short white kilt. Five lines of inscription on the base of the statue provide Kai's titles, including the 'Steward of the Great Estate.'

Kai's daughter can be seen sitting at her father's left leg; she is wearing a wig and a fitted white dress, as well as a wesekh-collar of three bands. Kai's son can be seen standing, embracing the right leg of his father. He holds a finger to his mouth – a sign of childhood – and has short, black hair.

page 27 | *The Dwarf Perniankhu* | *JE 98944; Basalt; H. 48cm; 4th Dynasty, Old Kingdom; Giza; Ground Floor, Room 42*
pages 28-29 | *The Statue of Kai* | *JE 99128; limestone; H. 58cm; 5th Dynasty, Old Kingdom; Giza; Ground Floor, Hall 46*

**JE 98945**

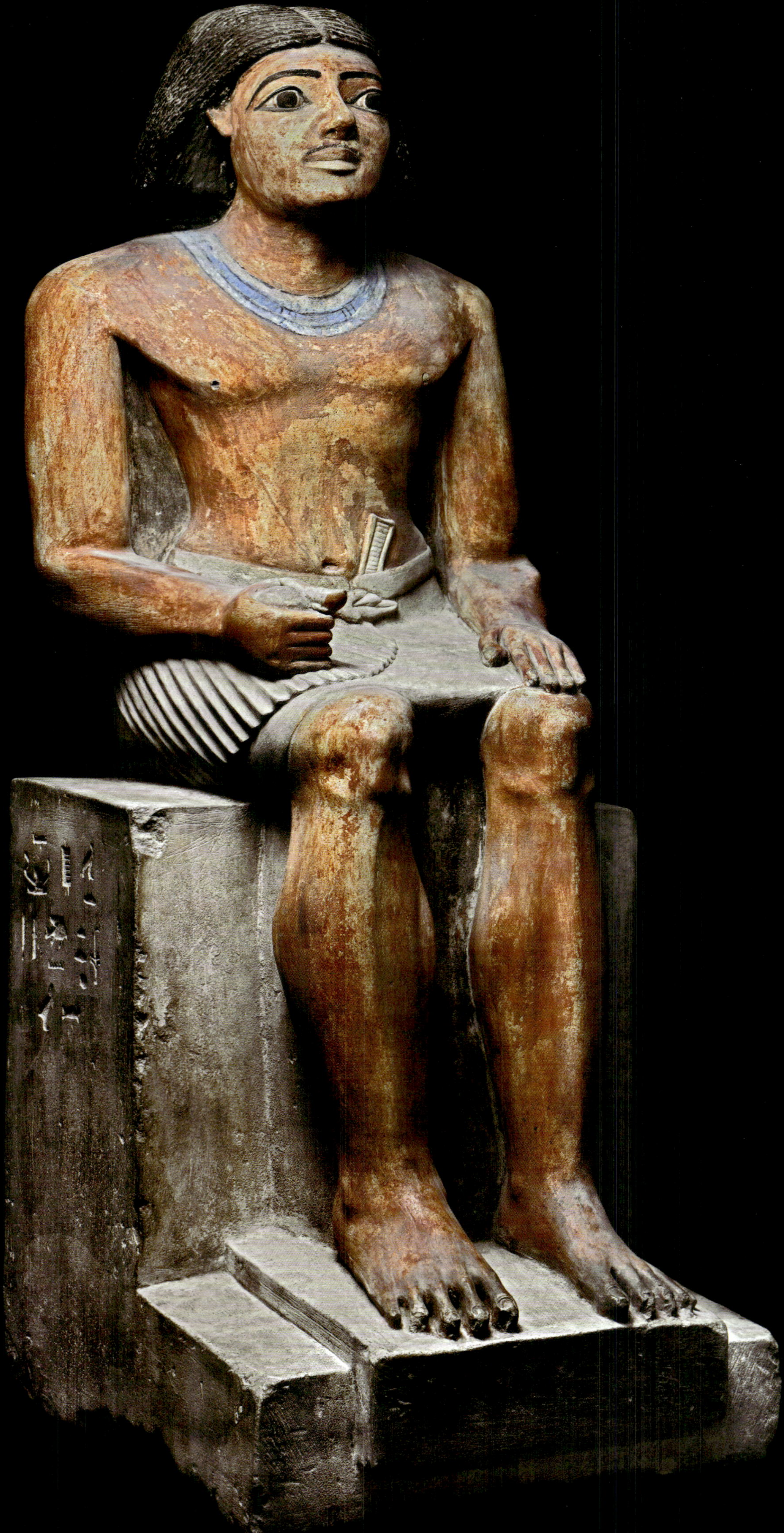

# The Four Statues of Intyshedu

*JE 98945; H. 75cm; JE 98946; H. 40.5cm; JE 98947; H. 32cm; JE 98948; H. 31cm; painted limestone; 4th Dynasty, Old Kingdom; Giza; Ground Floor, Room 32*

My other favourite group of statues was found amongst the tombs of the pyramid builders at Giza – the four statues of Intyshedu.These four statues all represent the same person at different stages in life. When I excavated the tomb in the upper cemetery, I saw a niche in the wall; it was blocked up with limestone and mud bricks, except for a small hole and, within, I could see the eyes of a statue looking out at me. When we removed the blocks, we discovered that there was not just one statue, but four: in the middle was the main, large, seated statue, to its right was another seated statue, while to its left was another seated statue and a standing statue. All bore the name Intyshedu. As the Egyptians believed in arranging their art according to symmetry, it seemed odd to me that a large, central statue would have two statues to one side and only one to the other. Then, we found the remains of a wooden statue on the right, which had entirely disintegrated. Thus, there were originally five statues: the central statue, most likely along with a standing and seated figure to either side.

The main statue depicts Intyshedu on a backless chair, wearing a black wig. The eyes and eyebrows are not symmetrical, and a thin black line represents his moustache. The body is of a strong man; his left hand rests on his knee, while he holds a folded cloth in his right hand. Below, he wears a short white kilt, tied with a belt. On the right side of the chair he is identified as, 'the Overseer of the Boat of the Goddess Neith, the King's Acquaintance, Intyshedu.'

The statue found to the left of the main statue is smaller in size and again shows Intyshedu seated on a backless chair. He wears a flared wig, common in the Old Kingdom, and has large, wide-spaced eyes. He wears a wesekh (broad) collar around his neck, painted with three rows of beads, coloured blue and white. His hands are placed on his knees, while his right hand holds a folded cloth. He is wearing a white kilt, tied with an elaborate knot at the waist. This statue appears to depict Intyshedu in his youth.

The third statue was also found to the left of the main statue. Here Intyshedu is shown standing with his left leg striding forward, he wears a short tied white kilt, and holds a folded cloth in each hand. He has a short wig on his head and both eyes and eyebrows slope downwards. His moustache is, again, indicated by a thin black line above the lip and he wears a broad collar but, this time, of white and blue beads.

The statue found to the right of the central figure also shows Intyshedu seated on a backless chair, his two hands on his lap. He wears a black wig, which reaches down to the shoulders. The face is circular and well defined. He wears a broad collar of white and blue. He holds a folded cloth in his right hand and he is wearing a short white kilt.

pages 30, 32-33 | *The Statues of Intyshedu* | *JE 98945; H. 75cm; JE 98946; H. 40.5cm; JE 98948; H. 31cm; painted limestone; 4th Dynasty, Old Kingdom; Giza; Ground Floor, Room 32*

CVV

32

98948

# III
# The Ground Floor of the Museum

# The Entrance Area and Predynastic Period

*Upon entering the museum you will find yourself in a small entrance area. In front of you is the Predynastic Room, and to your left is the first section of the Old Kingdom statuary halls. However, if you briefly look to your right you will be able to see a very important piece.*

## 1. The Rosetta Stone

*Replica; Ground Floor, Hall 48; original in the British Museum, London*

This is a replica of the original object in the British Museum, nevertheless it is very important for us to understand the story of the Rosetta Stone. When I became the head of Antiquities in 2002 I went to give a lecture at the British Museum, and they held a party among the statues. I told everyone present that I was the only one in the world who could speak to the statues, and that Ramesses II and Tuthmosis III were telling me that they missed Egypt incredibly. They told me that although they wanted to go home, they knew that they had to stay in the UK in order to tell people about how the Egyptians ruled the world with *maat* - justice. I added, however, that both had said to me, 'Zahi, you must tell them that you have to take the Rosetta stone with you, because it's the icon of our identity.' It was a joke, of course, but the press took hold of it and it started a war.

After returning to Egypt I wrote a letter to the British Museum, asking for the Rosetta stone to be present at the opening of the Grand Egyptian Museum as a symbol of the cooperation between us. However, they replied by saying that under British law they needed to know the security situation at the new museum before anything could be sent. Still, I truly believe that masterpieces of Egyptian art should be in their homeland; I am not asking for the return of all the artefacts outside of Egypt, just six specific important pieces– the Bust of Nefertiti in Berlin, the Rosetta stone in the British Museum, the Dendera Zodiac at the Louvre, the Statue of Hemiunu in Hildesheim, the bust of Ankhaf in Boston, and the Statue of Ramesses II in Turin.

The Rosetta Stone was found by the French in 1799 in Rosetta; it bears inscriptions from the priests of Egypt to King Ptolemy V written in two languages in three scripts – demotic, hieroglyphic and Greek. Many people tried to decipher the inscriptions, with one of the most important attempts made by the English scholar Thomas Young; it was not until 1822, however, when Champollion gave his speech at the Sorbonne explaining how he had managed to read the royal names in the cartouches, that the breakthrough occurred. Champollion was able to show us the ancient Egyptian language for the first time, leading to the birth of the academic discipline of Egyptology. The Rosetta Stone is thus very important in the history of Egyptology, and we hope that one day visitors to Egypt will be able to see the original in the Egyptian Museum.

Now, I would like to take you on a tour of the masterpieces of the Egyptian Museum. This tour could take one hour, or more than three hours, depending on how long you spend viewing each artefact. Let us start our adventure in the Predynastic Period.

# A Brief History of the Predynastic and Early Dynastic Period

*Prehistoric Period – c.2686 BC*

*The Prehistoric and Predynastic displays in the Egyptian Museum are the first objects that you will see when you enter the museum. The Prehistoric Period is divided into the Old, Middle and New Stone Ages. The New Stone Age, or Neolithic, is the period when we first begin to see the emergence of Egyptian civilisation. At this time, many major prehistoric sites, such as Beni Salama, Helwan, and areas of the Faiyum develop. There is then the Chalcolithic Period (Copper Stone Age), which takes us from the Badari Culture of Middle Egypt through Naqada phases I, II, III, and then into Dynasty 0. The historical Pharaonic period proper then begins with the Archaic or Early Dynastic Period, comprising the 1st and 2nd Dynasties.*

*Hall 43*

## 2. The Narmer Palette

*JE 32169; schist; H. 64cm; Dynasty 0, Early Dynastic Period; Hierakonpolis; Ground Floor, Hall 43*

The Narmer palette could be the first military document in history. It comes from a period when Egypt was still divided into two kingdoms – north and south. In the northern kingdom, the king wore the Red Crown, symbolised by the Papyrus plant, with the goddess Nekhbet as his protector. In the southern kingdom, the king wore the White Crown, symbolised by the Lotus, with the goddess Wadjet as his protector. According to legend King Menes unified the country, and some scholars have associated him with Narmer due to the imagery present on this palette; however, it is more likely that King Hor-Aha should be seen as the historical unifier of Egypt, with Narmer being the last king of Dynasty 0.

The Narmer palette has carved decoration on both sides. On one side we see the king wearing the White Crown, holding an upraised mace in his right hand, while in his other hand he holds an enemy by the hair, ready to smite him. A clump of papyrus is also in front of him, with a prisoner's head tied by the nose. Behind the king is the royal sandal-bearer; his name is written with the symbol of a flower and he holds a vessel for purification in his right hand. In the lower register we see two fallen foreigners, while at the top of the palette are two images of Hathor – human-faced cows with curling horns. The king's name – Narmer – is written in the serekh (symbol of the palace) in the top-middle of the piece. On the reverse side a representation of the king's victory can be seen in the second register, below the two images of Hathor and the name of Narmer. The king, this time wearing the Red Crown of Lower Egypt, walks in procession, his sandal-bearer again behind him. People carrying poles topped with standards, representing Narmer's victory, walk before them. At the far right of this register can be seen two rows of defeated enemies, their decapitated heads placed between their legs. In the register below are two long-necked mythological animals, which represent the north and the south. Two men are controlling the creatures, symbolising the control of the Two Lands, while the intertwined heads represent unification. In the bottom register the king is presented as a strong bull, destroying a fortress and defeating an enemy.

page 39 | **2. *The Narmer Palette*** | *JE 32169; schist; H. 64cm; Dynasty 0, Early Dynastic Period; Hierakonpolis; Ground Floor, Hall 43*

38

## 3. The Head of a God

*JE 97472; clay; H. 10cm; Maadi Era, Predynastic Period; Merimda Beni Salama; Ground Floor, Hall 43*

This is a truly beautiful piece - a crudely modelled Neolithic head, thought to be of a god, from the site of Beni Salama in the Western Delta; I excavated here in 1977 as a young man, and discovered much new important evidence about the site, especially regarding predynastic food production.

This piece could represent the first time that the Egyptians tried to model a human head in history. It has two holes for the eyes; a nose and a mouth. There is also a large hole below the head, which may have been for hanging the piece – perhaps outside a temple or a chapel – or for attaching it to a pole. There are also many holes around the face that may have been used to create a beard from feathers.

## 4. Board Game Pieces

*JE 44918 A-F; ivory; max. H. 3.5cm; 1st Dynasty, Early Dynastic Period; Abu Roash; Ground Floor, Hall 43*

These six board game pieces were associated with a game called Mehen 'coil,' because it was played on a circular limestone board that took the form of a coiled snake, its skin divided into squares. Three playing pieces represent recumbent lions, and three recumbent lionesses.

## 5. The Hemaka Discs

*JE 70164 (hunting scene); steatite; D. 9.5cm; JE 70162 (geometric decoration); schist, limestone; D. 10cm; JE 70160 (two birds); limestone; D. 9.6cm; 1st Dynasty, Early Dynastic Period; Saqqara; Ground Floor, Hall 43*

Hemaka, who lived during the 1st Dynasty, was a treasurer and vizier. His tomb contained many funerary objects, with decorated pieces made of stone, copper, ivory, and wood. These particular objects – known as the Hemaka discs - were found in 1936 by the Egyptologist Walter Emery inside a wooden box; we do not know their purpose, but Emery suggested that they may have been used for weaving, although they may have been used as part of a game. One of the examples bears a hunting scene, showing two dogs and two gazelles, another shows two birds, while the final example displays geometric patterns.

## 6. Two Vessels for Khasekhemwy

*JE 34941; carnelian, dolomite, gold; H. 4.2cm; JE 34942; dolomite, gold; H. 7.2cm; 2nd Dynasty, Early Dynastic Period; Abydos; Ground Floor, Hall 43*

These two vessels were discovered in King Khasekhemwy's tomb at Abydos. The top of each is covered with a thin layer of gold leaf, sealing the vessel. They represent vessels used in life, but were intended to last for eternity and so were made from materials that would not degrade over time.

**JE 34941**

**JE 34942**

**JE 41247**

44

JE 70164

## 7. The Libyan Palette

*JE 27434; schist; H. 19cm; Naqada III, Predynastic Period; Abydos; Ground Floor, Hall 43*

Only the lower part of this palette, which is inscribed on both sides, can be seen here. On one side are three rows of animals walking one behind the other. In the upper register, oxen with white eyes are walking together, the muscles of their legs clearly defined - a typical feature of the art of this period. In the middle register are donkeys, and in the third register are rams. Each row ends with a young animal. In the lowest register, trees and plants representing the environment can be seen. The word tehenu is on the lower right side; this refers to the Libyans of the Western Delta, and so indicates that these animals may have been taken by the Egyptians following a war.

On the reverse side of the palette we see the square shapes of seven fortresses. Above each is a symbol of a god or goddess, such as a hawk, lioness, and scorpion; all are symbols of power and kingship, and each holds a hoe, performing the foundation ceremony for the town or fortress.

## 8. The Gerza Slate

*JE 43103; Schist; H. 15cm; Naqada II, Predynastic Period; Gerza; Ground Floor, Hall 43*

Slate palettes, such as this, appear in burials during the Badarian Phase of the Predynastic Period. Their earliest forms are very simple, lacking any decoration, but by Naqada I symbols such as fish, birds, hippos, lions, and human shapes begin to appear. In Naqada II, the palettes become more detailed, and perhaps became associated with religious ritual and magic. After this the Egyptians began to use palettes to commemorate important events, and placed them in temples. This particular palette depicts the goddess Hathor, who is represented in the form of a cow. Stars can be seen around her head, displaying her cosmological significance. There is a hole to hang the palette.

pages 48-49 | *7. The Libyan Palette* | *JE 27434; schist; H. 19cm; Naqada III, Predynastic Period; Abydos; Ground Floor, Hall 43*
page 47 | *8. The Gerza Slate* | *JE 43103; Schist; H. 15cm; Naqada II, Predynastic Period; Gerza; Ground Floor, Hall 43*

46

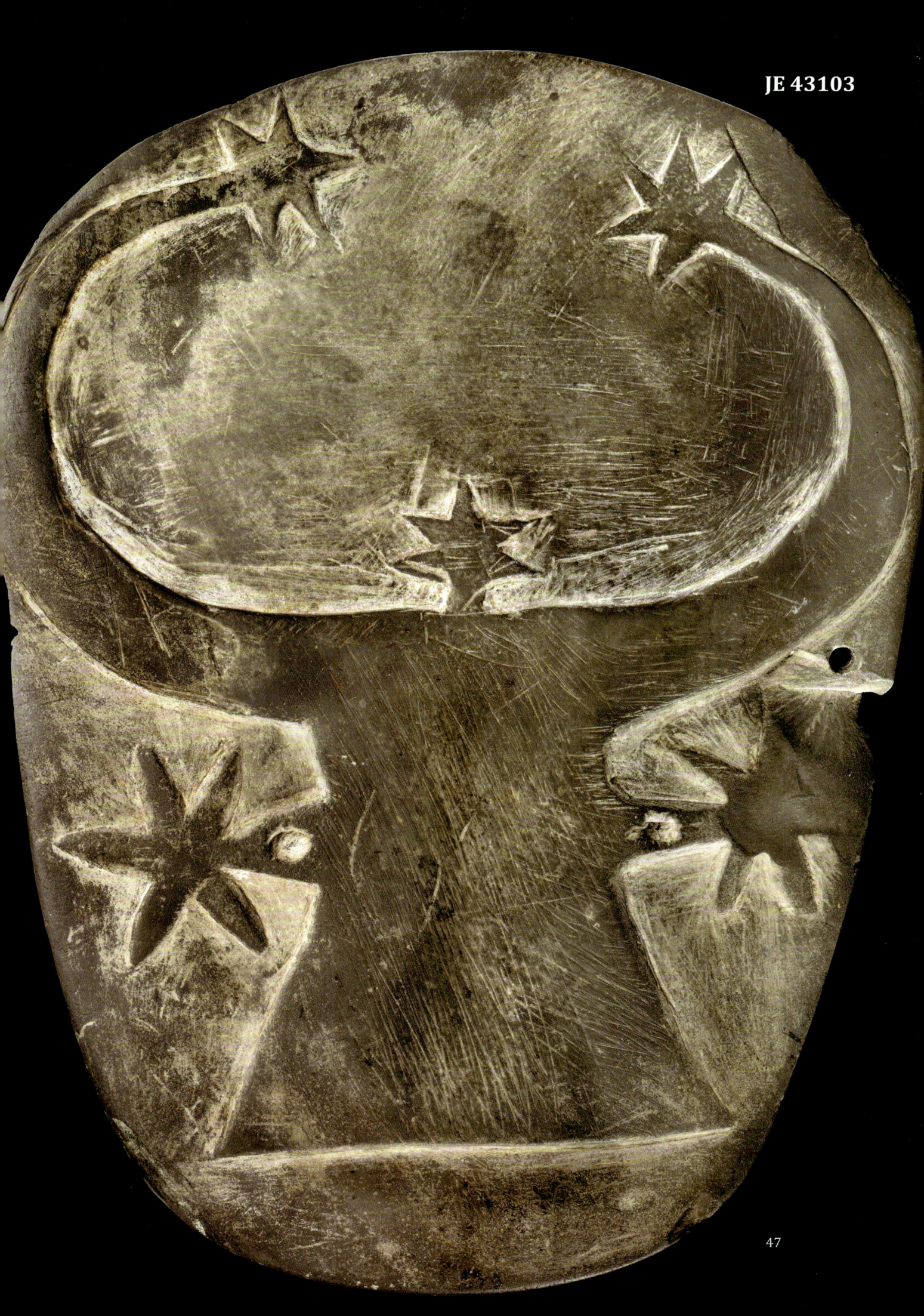

JE 27434

49

## 9. A Pottery Vessel with Coloured Decoration

*JE 64910; painted pottery; H. 21cm; Naqada II, Predynastic Period; unknown provenance; Ground Floor, Hall 43*

During the Naqada II phase of the Predynastic Period, geometric shapes are used to decorate pottery, as well as images of humans, animals, birds, boats, and plants. On this vessel a large boat with two cabins can be seen, along with forty oars. A standard rises above one of the cabins, which may be the symbol of a Nome (regional) goddess. Below, a group of nine ostriches – four on one side, and five on the other – can be seen. Their long necks and legs are clearly visible. Lines of plants can be seen beside them. On the other side of the vessel there is another scene of a boat, and we can see that the ancient artist used wavy lines to represent water.

## 10. A Flint Knife with a Golden Handle

*JE 34210; wood and flint; H. 30.6cm; Naqada II; Predynastic Period; Gebelein; Ground Floor, Hall 43*

It is likely that this knife was not used in daily life, but rather for religious purposes. The handle is made of wood, and the knife is made of flint. On one side three feminine shapes can be seen, perhaps depictions of dancers, while on the reverse side there are scenes of boats.

## 11. A Double Vessel

*JE 41247; pottery; H. 7.6 cm; Naqada I, Predynastic Period; Abydos; Ground Floor, Hall 43*

This vessel can be dated to the Naqada I phase of Egypt's Predynastic Period. Pottery played a very important role in defining the chronology of the Predynastic Period; the Egyptologist Flinders Petrie developed a sequence of how Predynastic pottery changed over time after looking at the pottery in different Predynastic cemeteries. One of the typical forms of pottery found in the Predynastic Period is black-topped red-ware, which belongs to the Naqada I phase. These vessels were formed from coiled clay, then smoothed and covered with a red ochre slip. They were then fired upside down in the kiln, leading to the rim area becoming black.

page 51 | *9. Pottery Vessel with Coloured Decoration* | *JE 64910; painted pottery; H. 21cm; Naqada II, Predynastic Period; unknown provenance; Ground Floor, Hall 43*
page 51 | *10. A Flint Knife with a Golden Handle* | *JE 34210; wood and flint; H. 30.6cm; Naqada II; Predynastic Period; Gebelein; Ground Floor, Hall 43*
page 44 | *11. A Double Vessel* | *JE 41247; pottery; H. 7.6 cm; Naqada I, Predynastic Period; Abydos; Ground Floor, Hall 43*

**JE 64910**

64910

**JE 34210**

51

## 12. A Statue of King Khasekhemwy

*JE 32161; schist; H. 56.5cm; 2nd Dynasty, Early Dynastic Period; Hierakonpolis; Ground Floor, Hall 48*

As you leave the Predynastic Room, and before you enter the Old Kingdom statuary displays, be sure to view this statue of King Khasekhemwy, the last king of the 2nd Dynasty. This beautiful statue marks the beginning of art carved from hard stone; the king is shown seated on his throne, wearing the White Crown of Upper Egypt and a tight robe with long sleeves associated with the heb-sed ritual of royal renewal. His right arm is placed on his right leg, while his left hand reaches across to hold his right arm. Part of the right side of the king's head has been lost, but the remarkable beauty and quality of the carving is still evident.

## A Brief History of the Old Kingdom *(2686 – 2160 BC)*

*The Old Kingdom, also known as the Pyramid Age, begins with the 3rd Dynasty and ends with the 6th. Great developments in architecture and administration occurred during this time; significantly, the Step Pyramid of Djoser at Saqqara was the first monumental stone building in the world, and paved the way for future large-scale constructions. Pyramid construction became a national project, which in the process built Egypt; labour was organised on a grand scale and artisans and craftsmen developed their skills further. Politically the government was closely focused around the royal family, with royal sons and other relatives playing important roles in official positions. By the 5th Dynasty pyramids were being built on a much smaller scale; however, more emphasis was placed on the funerary complexes, and, by the end of the dynasty, the interior of the pyramids began to be decorated with the famous Pyramid Texts. As time progressed the power held by local district mayors, known as Nomarchs, began to increase, creating problems for the centralised government ruled by the king. This weakening of royal power would eventually lead to the collapse of the government and to Egypt being divided under the rule of various powerful local chieftains.*

## 13. The Priest Hetepdief

*JE 34557; red granite; H. 39cm; 3rd Dynasty, Old Kingdom; Memphis; Ground floor, Hall 43*

This statue is the oldest example of private statuary known from ancient Egypt. Hetepdief is shown sitting in the act of worship, his two hands placed on his knees in prayer. He wears a circular thick wig, and has a short neck, which will have made the statue less breakable. On his right shoulder can be seen the Horus names of three 2nd Dynasty Kings – Hetepsekhemwy, Raneb, and Nynetjer - which could indicate that he served each of these monarchs. The name of Hetepdief's father, Mery Djehuty, can be found on the base.

page 53 | *12. A Statue of King Khasekhemwy* | *JE 32161; schist; H. 56.5cm; 2nd Dynasty, Early Dynastic Period; Hierakonpolis; Ground Floor, Hall 48*
page 53 | *13. The Priest Hetepdief* | *JE 34557; red granite; H. 39cm; 3rd Dynasty, Old Kingdom; Memphis; Ground floor, Hall 43*

52

JE 34557

JE 32161

53

## 14. The Statue of Djoser

*JE 49158; painted limestone; H. 142 cm; 3rd Dynasty, Old Kingdom; Saqqara; Ground Floor, Hall 48*

Djoser was one of the great kings of ancient Egypt, who ruled during the 3rd Dynasty for twenty-nine years. It was during his reign that the Egyptians first began to use stone in a monumental way and created the first pyramid. This statue represents the king sitting on a low-backed throne, wearing a tripartite wig surmounted by the royal nemes-headdress. You can see Djoser's strength and power in his face. He wears the heb-sed robe, a ceremonial garment worn during a royal ritual of renewal held after thirty years of rule. In my opinion this festival was held to celebrate all that the king had accomplished, in order to transform him into a god. Djoser sits in a traditional royal pose found throughout Egyptian history: his left hand is placed upon his knee, while his right hand is held across his chest. The royal title of King of Upper and Lower Egypt can be seen on the base of the statue, along with images of the protector goddesses Nekhbet and Wadjet. This is followed by the king's Horus name, Netjerykhet.

## 15. The Wooden Panels of Hesire

*JE 28504; wood; H. 114cm; 3rd Dynasty, Old Kingdom; Saqqara; Ground Floor, Hall 47*

Altogether there were originally eleven wooden panels in the tomb of Hesire at Saqqara, only six now survive, each showing Hesire at a different age in life, wearing different costumes and with different equipment. This man held important positions, each described on these wooden panels, including Chief of the Royal Scribes, Mayor of Buto, and Overseer of Dentists.

These pieces display the conventional art style that had developed by the 3rd Dynasty, and is then found throughout Egyptian history; here, the face is shown from the side, while the shoulders and eye are shown as if seen from the front. Both legs and feet can be seen as Hesire strides forward. In his right hand he holds the sekhem-sceptre, while in his left he holds his scribal equipment and a staff. The artist has carefully tried to show Hesire's eyebrows and moustache, while both the details of his wig and kilt are finely carved. He also has a prominent nose and full lips.

page 54 | *14. Statue of Djoser* | *JE 49158; painted limestone; H. 142 cm; 3rd Dynasty, Old Kingdom; Saqqara; Ground Floor, Hall 48*
pages 56-57 | *15. The Wooden Panels of Hesire* | *JE 28504; wood; H. 114cm; 3rd Dynasty, Old Kingdom; Saqqara; Ground Floor, Hall 47*

56

## 16. Figurine of a Woman making Beer

*JE 66624; painted limestone; H. 28cm; 5th Dynasty, Old Kingdom; Giza; Ground Floor, Hall 47*

This female figure is presented in the act of making beer, kneading dough in a strainer over a large jar. She wears a collar made of beads, and a long skirt below her naked torso. She is also wearing a wig, as it is possible to see her real hair beneath. She has an expressive face, and looks almost as if she is speaking to someone standing in front of her. The proportions of the body are not correct – notably she has large hands, although this may have been done on purpose to emphasise the woman's strength as she kneads the dough.

Servant statues, such as this one, played an important role in private tombs. Nobles and officials wanted to enjoy all the good aspects of this life in the next one; part of this was ensuring that servants would continue to work for them, and so they placed these statuettes in their burials to magically perform certain functions.

## 17. A Statue of Man Plucking a Goose

*JE 72232; painted limestone; H. 28cm, 5th Dynasty, Old Kingdom; Giza; Ground Floor, Hall 47*

This man is shown with a wide mouth, a thin moustache, and a red colour to his body. His hands are leaning on a small table, upon which is a slaughtered goose with a long neck.

## 18. Statue of King Raneferef

*JE 98171; painted limestone; H. 35cm; 5th Dynasty, Old Kingdom; Abu Sir;  Ground Floor, Hall 47*

Many objects were found in the funerary complex of King Raneferef, including numerous seals and this fragmentary statue of the king. Raneferef is shown sitting on a throne, wearing a wig, and with his right hand holding a sceptre across his chest. He is presented in a youthful manner with a round face, and wearing a short collar. The god Horus, in the form of a falcon, can be seen behind his head. I believe that if this statue had been found complete it would have been accorded the same status as the famous statue of Khafre.

## 19. The First Triad of Menkaure

*JE 46499; diorite; H. 96cm; 4th Dynasty, Old Kingdom; Valley Temple of Khafre, Giza; Ground Floor, Hall 47*

George Reisner discovered five complete triad statues of Menkaure in the King's Valley Temple at Giza. Three of these are now in the Egyptian Museum, while two are in Boston. Here the king can be seen standing, the muscles of his body well defined, wearing the White Crown of Upper Egypt, a false beard, and a short kilt. His left leg strides forward, in the conventional manner. The goddess Hathor, to his right, holds his hand, identifiable by the cow's horns and sun-disc that surmount her wig, and by the inscription below, which reads, 'Hathor, Lady of the Sycamore Tree in all her places.' To his left stands a personification of the Diospolis Parva Nome (district) of Egypt, herself identifiable by the standard above her head.

256

JE 40678

JE 40679

JE 46499

JE 30810

## 20. The Second Triad of Menkaure

*JE 40678; diorite; H. 93cm; 4th Dynasty, Old Kingdom; Valley Temple of Khafre, Giza; Ground Floor, Hall 47*

In this second triad statue on display, we see Menkaure in the centre, accompanied by Hathor on his right, standing with her hands at her sides. The personification of the Theban Nome stands to his left, presented as a short man with his left leg advancing forward, and his arms down by his sides. As with the other Nome personification described above, he is identifiable by the standard above his head. The king's beard has broken off.

## 21. A Third Triad Statue of Menkaure

*JE 40679; diorite; H. 93cm; 4th Dynasty, Old Kingdom; Valley Temple of Khafre, Giza; Ground Floor, Hall 47*

This piece, similar to those already described above, shows the king accompanied by Hathor and a Nome Goddess. This time, however, they both take him by the arm, and the Nome presented is that of Cynopolis.

## 22. The Statue of Urkhui

*JE 72221; limestone, H. 35cm; 6th Dynasty, Old Kingdom; Giza; Ground Floor, Hall 47*

Although incomplete due to damage, this is a very beautiful piece. The face is realistically carved, with eyes that seem alive, even though they lack the precious stones and inlays that would normally be present to add detail.

## 23. The Head of Userkaf

*JE 90220; green schist; H. 45cm; 5th Dynasty, Old Kingdom; Abu Sir; Ground Floor, Hall 47*

This masterpiece represents well the idealistic art style of the Old Kingdom because if you look at it closely it resembles the statues of Menkaure, already discussed above. Userkaf built his pyramid at Saqqara, but he also built a sun temple at Abu Sir, from where this colossal head, which likely originally belonged to a large statue, was excavated. The king can be seen wearing the Red Crown of Lower Egypt, which is rare in Old Kingdom statuary; the carving of the face is expertly done, with even the king's moustache carefully shown.

## 24. The Porter of the Basket of Niankhpepi

*JE 30810; wood; H. 36.4cm; 6th Dynasty, Old Kingdom; Meir, Asyut; Ground Floor, Hall 47*

This is a beautiful servant statue. He has wide eyes, that make him seem alive, a short kilt, and his left leg is striding forward. A bag is tied to his back by a strap around his neck, and he holds a beautiful box in his right hand.

JE 90220

JE 72221

JE 87805

JE 87807

## 25. The Family of Neferherenptah called Fifi

*JE 87804 (Fifi); H. 65cm; JE 87806 (Satmeret); H. 53cm; JE 87805 (Tesen); H. 37cm; JE 87807 (Meretites); H. 39cm; painted limestone; 5th Dynasty, Old Kingdom; Giza; Ground Floor, Hall 46*

These four statues were made for the ka (a form of the soul) of each member of Neferherenptah's family. Neferherenptah himself, who was also known as Fifi, had been a Lector Priest in the cults of Khafre and Menkaure. He can be seen here standing in a conventional pose; his arms are close by his sides, and his left leg is striding forward. He wears a short kilt, a painted collar, and a wig. His musculature is well defined. Beside him we can see his wife, Satmerit, who stands wearing a beautiful sleeveless white dress, that carefully follows the shape of her body. She wears a wig, but her real hair can be seen beneath on her forehead. She also wears an elaborate collar. Their children Tesen and Mererites are seated on backless chairs.

## 26. The Statue of a Priest called Khaemked

*CG 119; plastered and painted limestone; H. 42cm; 5th Dynasty, Old Kingdom; Saqqara; Ground Floor, Hall 46*

This is one of many statues found in the tomb of the Treasurer Urirni at Saqqara. It depicts Urirni's Funerary Priest, Khaemked, kneeling in a position of worship, clasping his hands on his knees, wearing a short kilt, tied with a belt. A copper frame emphasises his eyes, while his pupils are inlaid with obsidian. Overall, he projects an attitude of peace and calm. This is the most beautiful statue found in the tomb, even more so than those of the tomb owner himself.

## 27. A Reserve Head

*JE 46216; limestone; H. 19.5cm; 4th Dynasty, Old Kingdom; Giza; Ground Floor, Hall 46*

So-called reserve heads, such as this piece, were placed in the substructure of tombs of the 4th Dynasty. This particular piece was made for a member of the royal family of Khafre. They are not found in the later Old Kingdom, or in any subsequent periods of Egyptian history. There are many arguments as to why the Egyptians used them, ranging from their being realistic representations of the deceased, to them being models to create funerary masks. Others say that they were made for the soul to properly recognise the body in the afterlife, used as substitutes for the mummy or statues.

I was lucky to find one of these pieces myself during my excavations at the tombs of the workmen at Giza; it is an unusual piece because the ears are still intact, whereas the majority of reserve heads have broken ears. It has a hole in the neck too, which is also unusual. It is likely that the piece I found was unfinished and left over from the workshop, for the ears would surely have been broken off if it had been used.

## 28. The Statue of Kai

*JE 99128; limestone; H. 58cm; 5th Dynasty, Old Kingdom; Giza; Ground Floor, Hall 46*

Please see the 'my favourite objects in the museum' chapter for information about this piece.

pages 68, 70-71 | **25. The Family of Neferherenptah called Fifi** | *JE 87804 (Fifi); H. 65cm; JE 87806 (Satmeret); H. 53cm; JE 87805 (Tesen); H. 37cm; JE 87807 (Meretites); H. 39cm; painted limestone; 5th Dynasty, Old Kingdom; Giza; Ground Floor, Hall 46*
page 73 | **26. The Statue of a Priest called Khaemked** | *CG 119; plastered and painted limestone; H. 42cm; 5th Dynasty, Old Kingdom; Saqqara; Ground Floor, Hall 46*
page 72 | *27. A Reserve Head* | *JE 46216; limestone; H. 19.5cm; 4th Dynasty, Old Kingdom; Giza; Ground Floor, Hall 46*

JE 87806

70

JE 87804

71

## 29. Scenes from the Tomb of Nefermaat

*JE 43809 A; H. 123cm; JE 43809 B; H. 138.5cm; limestone; 4th Dynasty, Old Kingdom; Meidum; Ground Floor, Hall 41*

These scenes, from the Tomb of Nefermaat at Meidum, represent the high artistic achievement of the Old Kingdom artists. Here we can see beautifully presented scenes of daily life, the vivid colour being the result of coloured paste inlays inserted into the reliefs. One scene shows a desert hunter, coming close to his prey, while dogs attack foxes in the register below. In another scene we see two men hunting birds, with the hieroglyphic word for 'trapping' written next to those that have been caught; below is a scene of ploughing.

## 30. Scenes from the Tomb of Kaemrehu

*CG 1534; painted limestone; H. 97cm; 5th Dynasty, Old Kingdom; Saqqara; Ground Floor, Hall 41*

This wall relief was originally found within the tomb of the Priest of the Pyramid of Niussere, Kaemrehu, at Saqqara. In my opinion it is one of the masterpieces of 5th Dynasty art, and one of the most beautiful Old Kingdom reliefs showing daily life. One scene, at the top left, shows a group of donkeys accompanied by three men, while to the right, farmers perform their daily work.

In the second register, on the left, there is a scene of the harvest depicting workmen recording what is being placed in vessels; one man is even counting using his fingers. Further to the right, there is a judgement scene: two men are being punished for tax offences, while a series of scribes record the events of the trial.

The third register depicts beer making; here the hieroglyphics present the Egyptians talking about their work, while further to the right there is a scene of bread making in which one of the workmen is telling the other to grind the grain carefully, while the other responds that he is working with all his strength. The final register shows scenes of different industries, such as carpenters at work, goldsmiths, and sculptors carving statues.

## *Room 42*

## 31. The Statue of Khafre

*JE 10062; diorite; H. 168cm; 4th Dynasty, Old Kingdom; Khafre's Valley Temple, Giza; Ground Floor, Room 42*

Please see 'my favourite objects in the museum' chapter for information about this piece.

## 32. The Dwarf Perniankhu

*JE 98944; basalt; H. 48cm; 4th Dynasty, Old Kingdom; Giza; Ground Floor, Room 42*

Please see 'my favourite objects in the museum' chapter for information about this piece.

page 75 | *29. Scenes from the Tomb of Nefermaat* | *JE 43809; limestone; two reliefs, H. 61.5cm and 62cm; 4th Dynasty, Old Kingdom; Meidum; Ground Floor, Room 41*
pages 76-77 | *30. Scenes from the Tomb of Kaemrehu* | *CG 1534; painted limestone; H. 97cm; 5th Dynasty, Old Kingdom; Saqqara; Ground Floor, Hall 41*

JE 43809 A-B

**CG 1534**

## 33. The False Door of Ika

*JE 72201; wood, H. 200cm; 5th Dynasty, Old Kingdom; Saqqara; Ground Floor, Room 42*

To the ancient Egyptians the false door was a point of communication between the world of the living and the world of the dead. Through these doors the deceased could receive offerings from the living, and magically pass between the offering chapel and the burial chamber. False doors are important sources of historical information as they typically record the names, titles, and family members of important officials.

At the top of this false door is a carving of the deceased, the Ruler of the Great House, Ika, with his wife, Iymeret, sitting in front of an offering table facing one another. Farther below we see Ika and his son within a deep niche. On the right side of the door, his wife, Iymeret, who holds the title Priestess of Hathor, can be seen smelling a lotus flower, and wearing a very tight dress. On the opposite side is her husband, wearing a short kilt, holding a staff in his left hand, and a sceptre in his right. Above both figures can be seen their names and titles. At the very top of the false door can be seen the standard offering formula found in every Egyptian tomb. Here it refers to offerings that the king gives to Anubis in front of the divine booth. By reading the full offering formula any visitor to the tomb would magically provide offerings for the deceased and his family. Running vertically along the left side of the door can be seen another offering to Anubis, stating that Ika will proceed on a good road, protected by the Great God. On the right side there is an offering which the king gives of bread, beer, and fowl on various festival days. This could be the earliest wooden false door found in Egypt.

## 34. The Sheikh el-Balad

*CG 34; wood; H. 112cm; 5th Dynasty, Old Kingdom; Saqqara; Ground Floor, Room 42*

This statue represents the Lector Priest Ka-aper. At the time of its discovery by Auguste Mariette, an unpopular mayor in the village had died, and when the local workmen looked into the eyes of this statue they believed that he had returned. Thus, Mariette dubbed it the Sheikh el-Balad, The Headman of the Village. The carving shows the artist's great skill: the life-like expression on the face, with his thick cheeks, is emphasised by the copper framed eyes, with quartz acting as the white of the eyes, and black paste acting as the pupils. These elements combined make it is easy to believe that this man is alive and standing there. It is truly a masterpiece.

## 35. The Seated Scribe

*JE 30272; painted limestone; H. 51cm; 5th Dynasty, Old Kingdom; Saqqara; Ground Floor, Room 42*

This statue of an unknown seated scribe is one of my favourite pieces in the museum. The scribe is shown sitting on the ground, resting an open papyrus roll on his thighs. He wears a black wig, and has inlaid eyes, made of quartzite within a copper frame. When I look at this statue I really feel that the scribe is waiting there for the command to begin writing.

## 36. A Copper Statue of Pepi I or Merenre

*JE 33035; copper; H. 65cm; 6th Dynasty, Old Kingdom; Hierakonpolis; Ground Floor, Hall 31*

This copper statue of King Pepi I, or his son Merenre, was discovered within a larger copper statue of Pepi I at Hierakonpolis. Both are considered masterpieces of copper statuary from ancient Egypt. The smaller statue presents the king striding forward with his left leg, and holding his arms close by his sides. He originally held objects in his hands – probably staffs or folded cloths – but these are now lost; also, a uraeus will originally have been found in the hole at the king's forehead, and a protective falcon would have been behind the head. The eyes are inlaid with limestone and obsidian, and he wears a tight fitting cap decorated with circular curls atop his round head. Although presented naked, the statue will originally have worn a kilt. The copper that forms this and the larger statue had corroded over the years, and so they were both recently restored by a German team.

## 37. Two Statues of Ranefer

*JE 10063 (short kilt); H. 178cm; JE 10064 (long kilt); H. 186; painted limestone; 5th Dynasty, Old Kingdom; Saqqara; Ground Floor, Hall 31*

These two life-size statues represent the High Priest of Ptah and Sokar at Memphis, Ranefer. In both he stands in the same position, with a large back pillar behind. His left leg is striding forward, while he holds folded cloths (symbols of nobility) tightly in his hands. The only difference between the two statues is that the kilt is different, and on one he is shown wearing a wig, while in the other he has short hair.

## 38. Relief of Sneferu in Sinai

*JE 38568; sandstone; H. 112.5cm; 4th Dynasty, Old Kingdom; Sinai (Wadi Maghara); Ground Floor, Hall 31*

This relief, made of sandstone, shows Sneferu on a large scale, smiting an enemy who kneels, pleading for mercy, before him. The god Horus can be seen opposite Sneferu, wearing the Double Crown of Upper and Lower Egypt, and standing upon a serekh which contains the king's Horus name - Nebmaat. Sneferu's further names and titles surround his image. The Sinai was an important source of turquoise and copper to the Egyptians. By smiting the enemies of the region Sneferu is performing one of the roles of the king - securing trade routes through the control of rebellious tribes.

JE 10063

38568

## 39. The Statue of Rahotep and his Wife Nofret

*CG 3 (Rahotep); H. 121cm; CG 4 (Nofret); H. 122cm; painted limestone; 4th Dynasty, Old Kingdom; Meidum; Ground Floor, Room 32*

These beautiful statues are two of the wonders of the Egyptian Museum. They are so lifelike that when Mariette's workmen came across them they screamed, and one of them is even said to have died of a heart attack. Prince Rahotep, who was the son of Sneferu, held many important titles, such as High Priest of Ra in Heliopolis, Overseer of Expeditions, and Overseer of the Army. Nofret holds the honorific title, One Known by the King. These titles are written on the chairs behind the seated figures. Rahotep is shown wearing a short kilt, with a heart-shaped amulet hanging around his neck. His right hand is held across his torso, while he holds a folded cloth in his left hand. His hair is cut short, and a thin moustache can be seen. The most beautiful feature of this statue are the inlaid eyes, which make Rahotep seem alive.

Nofret is wearing a dress with two straps, enveloped by a thin shroud. She crosses her arms across her belly below her cloak, with only her right hand emerging. Around her neck she wears a wide collar, consisting of many coloured beads. She also wears a wig, with her real hair visible below, and a beautiful crown above. These two statues show very clearly the colour conventions used in Egyptian art when depicting males and females; Rahotep's body is coloured a dark red, while Nofret's is a pale yellow. This is because men would go out to work in the sun, while women would stay inside.

## 40. The Dwarf Seneb and his Family

*JE 51280; painted limestone; H. 34cm; 4th or 5th Dynasty, Old Kingdom; Giza; Ground Floor, Room 32*

This statue of the dwarf Seneb and his family was found in a tomb in the Western Cemetery of Giza, next to the tomb of Perniankhu, whom I believe is likely the father of Seneb due to the close proximity of their burials. Seneb worked in the royal palace associated with the royal wardrobe, and was also Chief of the Dwarfs in the Palace; his position made him rich, as it is known that he owned thousands of cattle. This is one of the most beautiful group statues of the Old Kingdom; he is shown sitting cross-legged, with his hands joined across his chest. His wife sits to his left, holding him with her hands, and we can see a slight smile on her face. She wears a long dress with sleeves, and a wig. Their children can be seen standing below Seneb's crossed legs preserving the composition of the piece, as if Seneb's legs were hanging down, and adding to the sense of symmetry.

pages 90-91 | **39. The Statue of Rahotep and his Wife Nofret** | *CG 3 (Rahotep); H. 121cm; CG 4 (Nofret); H. 122cm; painted limestone; 4th Dynasty, Old Kingdom; Meidum; Ground Floor, Room 32*
page 89 | **40. The Dwarf Seneb and his Family** | *JE 51280; painted limestone; H. 34cm; 4th or 5th Dynasty, Old Kingdom; Giza; Ground Floor, Room 32*

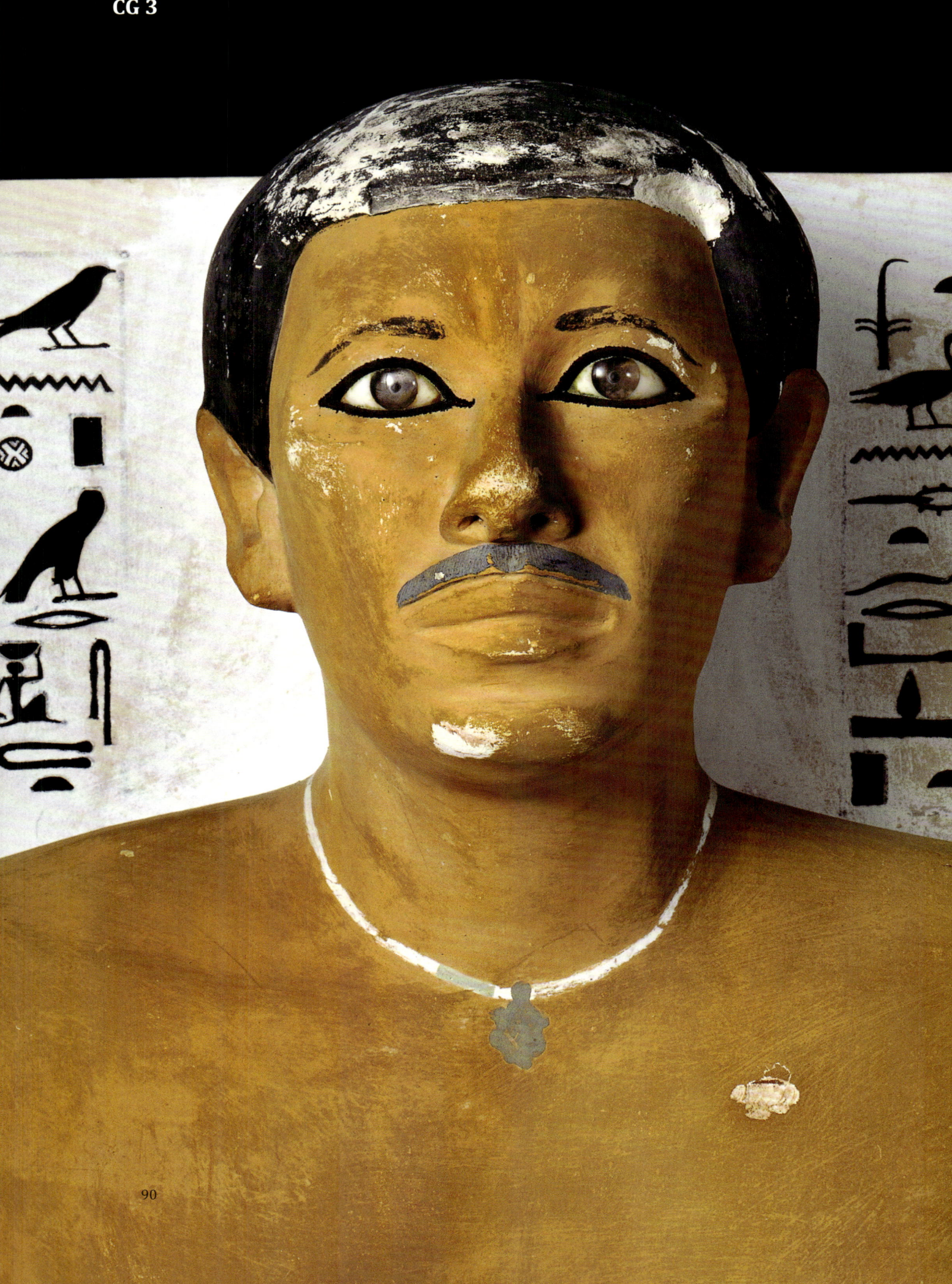

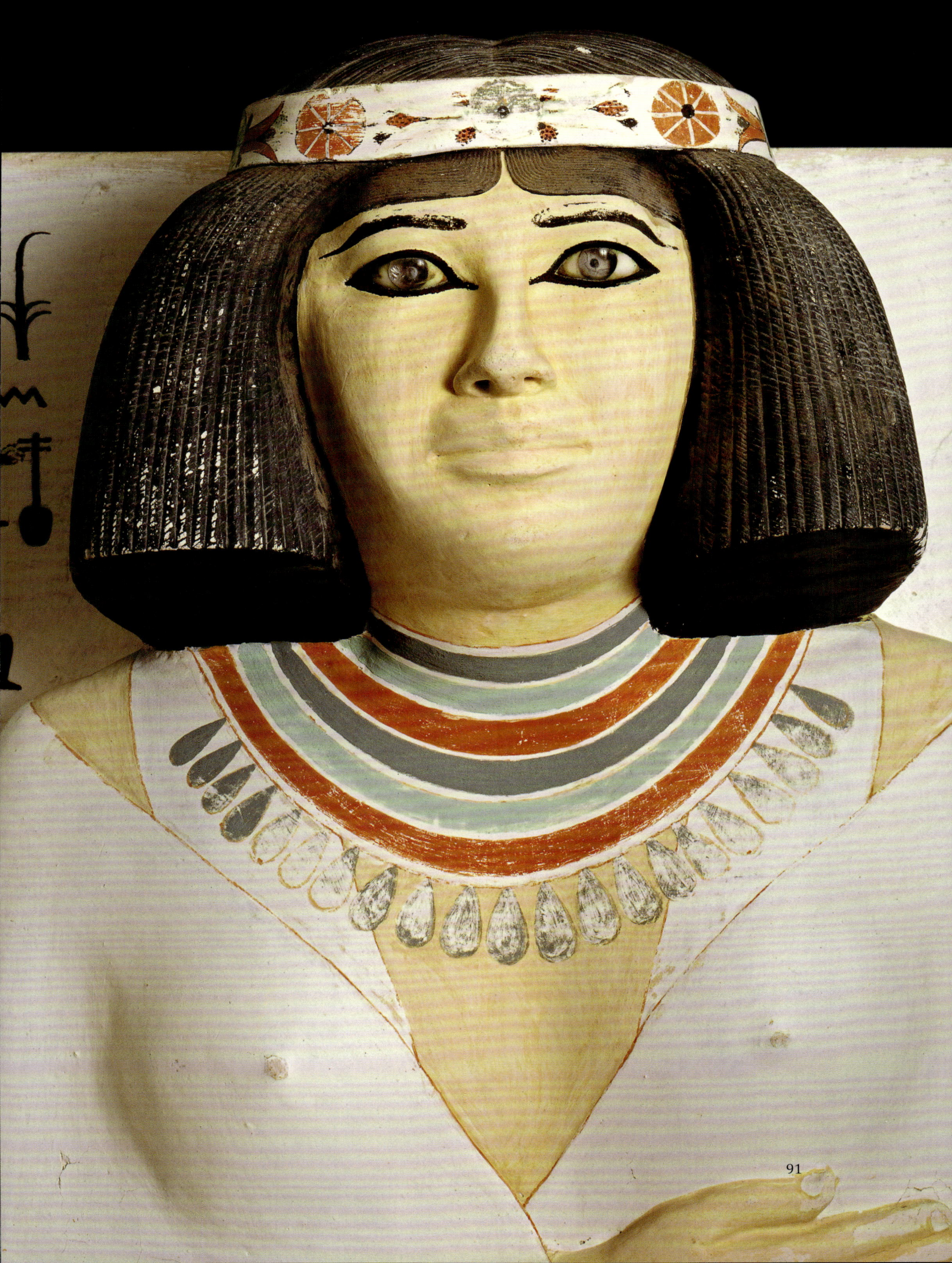

## 41. Statue of Mitri as a Scribe

*JE 93165; painted wood; H. 76cm; 5th or 6th Dynasty, Old Kingdom; Saqqara; Ground Floor, Room 32*

Mitri is known to have had many important religious and political positions, including Administrator of the Nome, and Priest of Maat. Here we see Mitri in a scribal position, which reflects his importance and education. He sits cross-legged on the ground, with his papyrus unrolled on his knees. Although much of the colour has been lost, we can still see the remains of it around the neck of the statue; however, it is the inlaid eyes that capture most people who see it.

Eleven statues connected to this man were found in his tomb; some represent him alone, while others show him with his wife. Of these eleven, five are in the Egyptian Museum, five are in the Metropolitan Museum of Art, New York, and one is in the Museum of Mediterranean and Near Eastern Antiquities, Stockholm.

## 42. A Scene of Fighting Boatmen

*JE 30191; limestone; L. 145cm; 5th Dynasty, Old Kingdom; Saqqara; Ground Floor, Room 32*

This scene is very realistic, showing two groups of fishermen fighting in their boats facing each other. This type of scene is common in the Old Kingdom, with the oldest example found in the tomb of Merysankh at Giza. The men fight with long sticks with forked ends, and as they do so their words to each other have been captured in the hieroglyphics accompanying the scene, reflecting the different moments in the fight. The aim of the fight was to throw the enemy into the water.

## 43. The Meidum Geese

*JE 34571; coloured gypsum, H. 27cm; 4th Dynasty, Old Kingdom; Meidum; Ground Floor, Room 32*

Six geese can be seen here, standing in two groups – one group to the right and one to the left – each consisting of three geese. The four central geese have their heads raised, while the final goose on each side is eating food from the ground. The geese are painted in exquisite detail, and the artist has shown great skill in creating a symmetrical composition. The artist was also keen to fill the spaces by drawing green grass, and also small flowers.

## 44. The Four Statues of Intyshedu

*JE 98945; H. 75; JE 98946; H. 40.5cm; JE 98947; H. 32; JE 98948; H. 31cm; painted limestone; 4th Dynasty, Old Kingdom; Giza; Ground Floor, Room 32*

Please see 'my favourite objects in the museum' chapter for information about this piece.

JE 93165

JE 30191

JE 34571

# A Brief History of the Hetepheres Funerary Assemblage

*(Ground Floor, Room 37)*

*George Reisner, from the Museum of Fine Arts, Boston, discovered the funerary equipment of Queen Hetepheres, wife of the 4th Dynasty King Sneferu and mother of King Khufu, in 1925. He was excavating on the east side of the Great Pyramid, but then went back to the States for a vacation, leaving his assistant behind to carry on his work. One day, the team's photographer was setting up his tripod, when one of its legs broke through into the ground, revealing the entrance to a hidden tomb shaft. Immediately a telegram was sent to Reisner to inform him of the discovery. He returned to Egypt and spent the next ten years excavating the shaft. Although Reisner originally argued that the queen was buried at Dashur, and had subsequently been moved to the shaft in Giza, it is now believed that she was originally buried in the northern subsidiary pyramid next to the Great Pyramid. Then, during the First Intermediate Period, when the priests found that the Old Kingdom monuments were being destroyed, they began to take all the objects out of the pyramid and hide them in the shaft.*

*When you enter this room you will see many examples of the exquisite furniture of the Old Kingdom. They are beautifully decorated, in a manner that does not seem out of place today, and display an artistic style that is very elegant and simple. The wood, used by the Egyptians to make their furniture, mostly came from Lebanon as wood is lacking in Egypt. They would also use ivory and leather to add ornamentation.*

## 45. The Sedan Chair

*JE 52372; wood, gold leaf, ebony; H. 52cm; 4th Dynasty, Old Kingdom; Giza; Ground Floor, Room 37*

This sedan chair could be extended to give the queen more space to relax. It is decorated around its edges with gold leaf. On both sides of the back rest can be see gold inscriptions written on an ebony strip, describing Hetepheres as the Mother of the King of Upper and Lower Egypt, and Daughter of Horus.

## 46. The Bed of Queen Hetepheres

*JE 53261; wood, gold leaf; L. 178cm; 4th Dynasty, Old Kingdom; Giza; Ground Floor, Room 37*

Scenes of bed manufacture are found in all periods of Egyptian history; we often see depictions of carpenters working with their tools, making simple beds from the low quality wood available to them. The wooden frame of Hetepheres's bed is covered in gold leaf, in the form of papyrus rolls. The bed is supported by four gilded wooden legs, carved in the form of lion's paws, which are attached to the main part of the bed by bands of leather. The bed slopes down towards the feet.

## 47. The Queen's Chair

*JE 53263; wood, gold leaf; H. 79cm; 4th Dynasty, Old Kingdom; Giza; Ground Floor, Room 37*

This chair displays the elegant simplicity that dominated fashion in the Old Kingdom. As was typical, the legs take the form of lion's paws and are attached separately. Each side of this chair is decorated with the sema tawy motif, which symbolises the unification of Upper and Lower Egypt.

page 97 | **45. The Sedan Chair** | *JE 52372; wood, gold leaf, ebony; H. 52cm; 4th Dynasty, Old Kingdom; Giza; Ground Floor, Room 37*
page 97 | **46. The Bed of Queen Hetepheres** | *JE 53261; wood, gold leaf; L. 178cm; 4th Dynasty, Old Kingdom; Giza; Ground Floor, Room 37*
page 97 | **47. The Queen's Chair** | *JE 53263; wood, gold leaf; H. 79cm; 4th Dynasty, Old Kingdom; Giza; Ground Floor, Room 37*

JE 53263

JE 52372

JE 53261

97

## 48. A Box Containing Bracelets

*JE 53265 (Box); wood, gold leaf; H. 21cm; JE 53266 – JE 53281 (Bracelets); silver, turquoise, lapis lazuli; 4th Dynasty; Old Kingdom; Giza; Ground Floor, Room 37*

We know that the ancient Egyptians loved to decorate themselves with jewellery, and that jewellery could have magical properties, which would help to protect those who wore it from hidden powers. As well as helping the living, the Egyptians also believed that jewellery could protect the deceased from evil, and so it was placed around the neck, hands, feet, or any part of the body seen as weak. This box contained twenty silver bracelets, covered with semiprecious stones, and is inscribed with hieroglyphs stating that Hetepheres is the mother of the King of Upper and Lower Egypt. It was restored by Ahmed Youssef, who also restored the Solar Boat of Khufu.

## 49. The Khufu Statuette

*JE 36143; ivory; H. 7.5cm; 26th Dynasty, Late Period; Abydos; Ground Floor, Room 37*

The Egyptologist Flinders Petrie was excavating in Abydos in 1903 when one of his workmen found the body of this statue, but without the head. After examining the piece Petrie realised that the break was recent, and so ordered his workmen to sift through all the sand in the area until the head was found.

This is the only surviving representation so far known of King Khufu, builder of the Great Pyramid. Despite the fact that the statue is very small the artist succeeded in expressing the power of the king. Khufu is identifiable here due to his Horus name being preserved on the piece. He sits on a throne, wearing the Red Crown of Lower Egypt, and a short kilt. In his right hand, over his chest, he holds a flail, while his left hand rests upon his left knee. This statue is typically cited as Old Kingdom in date, but after careful study, I believe it to be a 26th Dynasty copy of an Old Kingdom original.

## 50. A Statue of Sneferu

*JE 98943; limestone; H. 180cm; 4th Dynasty; Old Kingdom; Dashur; Ground Floor, Room 37*

This statue was found in pieces by Ahmed Fakhry in the Valley Temple of Sneferu at Dashur in 1954. My friend Rainer Stadelmann, who was the director of the German Institute from 1989 to 1998, was able to bring a German restoration team to work on the fragments, and now it has been reconstructed. The king can be seen wearing the White Crown of Upper Egypt, and a collar around his neck. He wears a short kilt, which is carved in detail and tied by a belt. The king's cartouche can be seen at the centre of the belt, along with the title King of Upper and Lower Egypt. He is striding forwards, but his left leg is entirely missing.

Sneferu was the first king of the 4th Dynasty; his reign was remarkable because of developments in foreign trade, major campaigns against Egypt's enemies, and because it was the first time that a true pyramid was built. It was once thought that Sneferu ruled for twenty-four years, but recent evidence now suggests that he ruled for fifty-four years.

99

JE 98943

# The Monuments of the Middle Kingdom

*A Brief History of the Middle Kingdom (c. 2055 – 1650 BC)*

*Modern scholars place the end of the Old Kingdom with the rise of the 7th Dynasty. The Old Kingdom's decline, however, had already begun during the reign of Pepi II, a 6th Dynasty king who ruled for 90 years. Little is known about the period of the 7th and 8th Dynasties, except that a series of kings ruled briefly from Memphis. Following this time, two influential families emerged and took control of the country; one based in Lower Egypt at Herakleopolis (Dynasty 9), and the other ruling from Coptos in Upper Egypt (Dynasty 10), later to be overpowered by the Intef family of Thebes. These ruling families fought amongst themselves until Montuhotep II, whose family ruled in Upper Egypt, was victorious and unified the Two Lands. This marks the beginning of the Middle Kingdom. Statuary from this period has been found in a wonderful state of preservation; from the statues of Senwosret I at Lisht, and the realistic statues of Senwosret III, to the statues of Amenemhat III expressing his peaceful persona.*

*Hall 26*

## 51. The Statue of Nebhepetre Montuhotep

*JE 36195; painted sandstone; H. 138cm; 11th Dynasty, Middle Kingdom; Deir el-Bahri, Luxor; Ground Floor, Hall 26*

Some scholars have argued that the First Intermediate Period, a time of crisis in Egypt, lasted roughly 100 years, until Nebhepetre Montuhotep (also referred to as Montuhotep II) unified the land and ruled over its people for 51 years. During that time, he built temples for the gods, developed agriculture, and erected his beautiful two-terraced temple at Deir el-Bahri in Thebes. This painted sandstone statue shows the king wearing the ceremonial heb-sed robe - connected to a festival celebrated after 30 years of rule in which the king proves his strength to rule. He is sitting on a throne wearing the Red Crown of Lower Egypt, and a curling false beard. His skin is painted black, representing both the fertile soil from the Nile, and the skin colour of Osiris, accentuating the king's association with the god. The king's arms are crossed over his chest, in a position also typically associated with Osiris. The statue has strong features and disproportionate legs, which has led some to believe that the king had elephantiasis. This is highly unlikely, however, as artists in ancient Egypt rarely represented physical deformities in royal statuary. Other scholars have argued that the artist lacked the necessary skills to produce elegant statues due to the artistic deterioration of the First Intermediate Period.

## 52. The Statue of Queen Nofret

*JE 37487; black granite; H. 165cm; 12th Dynasty, Middle Kingdom; Tanis; Ground Floor, Hall 26*

This statue of Queen Nofret, wife of Senwosret II, was found at the site of Tanis in the Delta during Auguste Mariette's excavation in 1860-1861. The queen, seated on a throne, has her right hand touching her knee, while her left hand is placed on her right arm. She wears a wig, later known as the Hathor wig, which ends over her breasts in two curls. The uraeus on her forehead is reduced in size. The queen has adopted typical Middle Kingdom iconography: her ears are disproportionately large, as are her face and limbs; her dress opens low on the chest, and she wears a very popular style of pectoral, as demonstrated by the numerous examples found in Middle Kingdom tombs.

page 103 | **51. The Statue of Nebhepetre Montuhotep** | *JE 36195; painted sandstone; H. 138cm; 11th Dynasty, Middle Kingdom; Deir el-Bahri, Luxor; Ground Floor, Room 26*
pages 104-105 | **52. The Statue of Queen Nofret** | *JE 37487; black granite; H. 165cm; 12th Dynasty, Middle Kingdom; Tanis; Ground Floor, Hall 26*

JE 36195

## 53. A Statue of a Vizier

*JE 36931; grey granite; H. 113cm; 12th Dynasty, Middle Kingdom; Karnak temple, Luxor; Ground Floor, Hall 21*

This granite statue of a vizier was discovered by Legrain during his 1904 excavations at the temple of Amun-Re at Thebes within a large pit known as the Karnak cachette. By the Middle Kingdom, officials had been granted permission to place their statues within temple precincts. This vizier, whose name remains a mystery, took advantage of this privilege in order to receive protection and help from the gods. He is seated on a backless chair with both hands on his knees. In his right hand, he holds a folded cloth, a sign of nobility. His round face bears a false beard, and he wears a long kilt tied at his chest, typical of his high-ranking position.

## 54. A Statue of Senwosret III

*TR 18.4.22.4; granite; H. 150cm; 12th Dynasty, Middle Kingdom; Deir el-Bahri, Luxor; Ground Floor, Hall 21*

This granite statue of King Senwosret III was discovered on the causeway leading to the Temple of Montuhotep II at Deir el-Bahri, Luxor, which was used as a processional way during the annual Beautiful Festival of the Valley. This masterpiece shows the king wearing the nemes-headdress with a uraeus at the forehead. Amazing skill has been shown in the rendering of the king's realistic facial expressions - his tired eyes, the bitter mouth, the forceful frowning, and the large ears. The tormented visage of the king reflects his new role and responsibility as administrator of Egypt, a result of the later 12th Dynasty kings' policies of expanding the Egyptian border further south, and of crushing the authority of independent Nomarchs in order to create a more powerful centralised government. His hands are placed on his kilt in a sign of piety toward the gods.

page 107 | **53. A Statue of a Vizier** | *JE 36931; grey granite; H. 113cm; 12th Dynasty, Middle Kingdom; Karnak temple, Luxor; Ground Floor, Hall 21*
page 107 | **54. A Statueof Senwosret III** | *TR 18.4.22.4; granite; H. 150cm; 12th Dynasty, Middle Kingdom; Deir el-Bahri, Luxor; Ground Floor, Hall 21*

TR 18.4.22.4

JE 36931

## 55. A Small Statue of King Senwosret I

*JE 44951; cedar wood; H. 56cm; 12th Dynasty, Middle Kingdom; Lisht; Ground Floor, Room 22*

This small wooden statue of King Senwosret I was discovered in the tomb of the Chancellor Imhotep, close to the king's pyramid at Lisht, during the Metropolitan Museum of Art's excavations in 1915. It was found within a hidden room in the enclosure wall of Imhotep's tomb, along with three more wooden objects: a model boat, a naos of Anubis, and a similar statue of King Senwosret I, now in the Metropolitan Museum, New York. This latter statue wears the Red Crown of Lower Egypt, as opposed to the example in the Egyptian Museum which wears the White Crown of Upper Egypt. Senwosret is presented here wearing a short kilt, painted white with red details. His skin is brown, and there is a hole under his chin, which could indicate the presence of a false beard. In his left hand, he holds the heka-sceptre, a symbol of royal authority, while in his right hand he probably held the sekhem-sceptre, a symbol of power.

## 56. The Statues of Senwosret I

*JE 31139; limestone; H. 200cm; 12th Dynasty, Middle Kingdom; Lisht; Ground Floor, Room 22*

A group of ten statues of King Senwosret I was found during the 1894 expedition of the French Archaeological Institute (IFAO) at Lisht in the Faiyum, buried in a hidden location north-east of the king's mortuary temple. Each statue shows the king seating on a backless throne holding a folded cloth, wearing the nemes-headdress, a short kilt, and sporting a false beard. Although all the statues look the same, they each differ slightly from one another. Notably, the decoration on the sides of the thrones changes: on five of the statues Nile gods can be seen tying a knot around the hieroglyphic sign for union, in reference to the unification of the Two Lands; while on the five remaining statues the Nile gods are replaced by images of Horus and Seth. On the upper base of three statues, the king stands on the Nine Bows, the traditional enemies of Egypt, thus restoring maat from chaos.

page 109 | **55. A Small Statue of King Senwosret I** | *JE 44951; cedar wood; H. 56cm; 12th Dynasty, Middle Kingdom; Lisht; Ground Floor, Room 22*
pages 110-111 | **56. The Statues of Senwosret I** | *JE 31139; limestone; H. 200cm; 12th Dynasty, Middle Kingdom; Lisht; Ground Floor, Room 22*

JE 44951

## 57. A Statue of Amenemhat III as a Priest

*JE 20001; black granite; H. 100cm; 12th Dynasty, Middle Kingdom; Crocodilopolis, Faiyum; Ground Floor, Hall 16*

This statue of Amenemhat III, of which only the torso remains, was discovered in 1862 by Auguste Mariette in the ancient capital of the Faiyum Oasis, known by the Greeks as Crocodilopolis. The king is dressed as a priest, evidenced by the leopard skin and paw over both shoulders. He has a heavy and unusual haircut and a real beard. One can still see where the false beard was once attached, as well as the hole for the missing uraeus. He is wearing the menat-collar. This statue shows highly individualistic facial features, which goes against the usual idealising tendencies.

## 58. A Double Statue of Amenemhat III as the Nile God

*JE 18221; grey granite; H. 160cm; 12th Dynasty, Middle Kingdom; Tanis; Ground Floor, Hall 16*

This double statue of Amenemhat III as Hapy, the Nile god, was discovered at Tanis, capital of the 21st Dynasty Pharaohs; however, the two male figures are clearly portraits of the 12th Dynasty king Amenemhat III. They are carved with perfect symmetry, offering fish, birds, and aquatic plants. Both wear heavy wigs with large braids, wide beards, and finely pleated kilts. This representation of the king as Hapy is a novelty in royal statuary.

## 59. A Statue of Amenemhat III in the Shape of a Sphinx

*JE 15210; grey granite; H. 150cm; 12th Dynasty, Middle Kingdom; Tanis; Ground Floor, Hall 16*

This statue of Amenemhat III was carved in the shape of a sphinx; joining a human head with a lion's body. This particular statue was part of a larger group of statues of the king, which were probably placed in the temple of Bastet, the cat goddess, at Bubastis in the Delta. Over time, however, the statues were usurped by numerous rulers – Nehesy, Ramesses II, Merenptah, and Psusennes – at which point they were transferred to different sites across Egypt. During the 21st Dynasty, this particular statue was taken by King Psusennes to Tanis, the new capital, where Auguste Mariette would later discover it. Despite the fact that all the royal cartouches have been usurped by later kings, scholars attribute this statue to Amenemhat III based on the strength, grandeur, and wisdom of the facial expressions - a typical feature of Amenemhat III's statuary. These features are amplified by the lion's mane, which replaces the nemes-headdress, and by the large ears. There is an inscription at the base.

# 60. The Ka-Statue of King Hor Auibre

*JE 30948; wood; H. 170cm; 13th Dynasty, Middle Kingdom; Dashur; Upper Floor, Hall 11*

This ka-statue of King Hor Auibre was found during de Morgan's 1884 excavation at Dahshur, within a tomb north of the pyramid complex of Amenemhat III. It was originally covered with painted stucco, which disintegrated to dust once it was exposed to air. The ancient Egyptians believed that their beings were composed of numerous parts; one such element was the Ka (the double or vital force). According to ancient Egyptian mythology, the ka was formed at the same time as the body on the God Khnum's potter's wheel. In order to survive after the body's physical death, the ka required the deceased's preserved corpse or a statue to inhabit, as well as a regular supply of food and drink. Thus, the ancient Egyptians did their best to preserve their human remains in order for the ka to live for eternity.

Ka-statues, much like the one, were placed inside the tomb, where they would receive goods placed on an offering table at the base of a false door, through which the ka could magically pass to receive energy from the food. This statue of King Hor Auibre has the hieroglyphic symbol for the Ka – two raised arms – above his head, emphasising its purpose. The king is completely naked, although traces of his belt and kilt can still be seen. He wears a tripartite wig that emphasises his ears, and a long false beard. His eyes are made of bronze, rock crystal and white quartz, producing a very realistic effect. His right hand probably held a sceptre, and his left hand a staff. His left leg can be seen striding forward.

page 117 | **60. The Ka-Statue of King Hor Auibre** | *JE 30948; wood; H. 170cm; 13th Dynasty, Middle Kingdom; Dashur; Upper Floor, Hall 11*

# The Monuments of the New Kingdom

## A Brief History of the New Kingdom (c. 1550 – 1069 BC)

*The New Kingdom is also known as the golden age of ancient Egypt. It begins with Ahmose, first king of the 18th Dynasty, who expelled foreign rulers known as the Hyksos from the north of Egypt. This then led to further military action into the Levant, and also into Nubia, in order to secure Egypt's borders and expand control. It is the period of the warrior pharaohs Tuthmosis III, Amenhotep II and Ramesses II, the Queen Hatshepsut, and the golden boy Tutankhamun, and a time of increased foreign relations and empire. It comprises the 18th – 20th Dynasties.*

*Hall 11*

## 61. The Head of Queen Hatshepsut

*JE 56259 - JE 56262; painted limestone; H.61cm; 18th Dynasty, New Kingdom; Deir el-Bahri, Luxor; Ground Floor, Hall 11*

Hatshepsut is the only female king to have ruled Egypt during a time of great unity and power. Other women had ruled as king, but only at the start of Intermediate Periods, such as Sobekneferu at the end of the 12th Dynasty. In my opinion Hatshepsut did not take the throne by force, rather Tuthmosis III, the true heir to the throne, was too young at the time of Tuthmosis II's death to take on the responsibility of the kingship, and someone needed to rule in his place. In the past there were theories that she had been murdered after becoming king, but when I discovered the mummy of Hatshepsut during the Egyptian Mummy Project we found that she had died of cancer.

Hatshepsut is famous for her beautiful mortuary temple at Deir el-Bahri in Luxor, from which this statue originates. The complete statue shows her in the form of Osiris. On this piece we can see that she is wearing the Red Crown of Lower Egypt, and that she has a very feminine face. We can also see that care has been taken to show her eyebrows, nose, and large eyes.

page 118 | **61. The Head of Queen Hatshepsut** | *JE 56259 and JE 56262; painted limestone; H.61cm; 18th Dynasty, New Kingdom; Deir el-Bahri, Luxor; Ground Floor, Hall 11*

119

## 62. The Bust of Tuthmosis III

*JE 90237; marble; H. 39.5cm; 18th Dynasty, New Kingdom; Deir el-Bahri, Luxor; Ground Floor, Room 12*
This beautiful bust was found at Deir el-Bahri in two pieces. The head that you see here is original, and was found during excavations in 1964, whereas the body is a cast of the original piece, now in the Metropolitan Museum of Art, New York. The colours of the royal nemes-headdress are very strong, and the king's eyes have been lined with black paint to give them extra emphasis. The king's nose and mouth are exquisitely carved.

## 63. A Statue of Sennefer and Senay

*JE 36574; granite; 120cm; 18th Dynasty, New Kingdom; Karnak Temple, Luxor; Ground Floor, Room 12*
Sennefer was an important noble during the reign of Amenhotep II; he was Mayor of Thebes, and responsible for the tribute taken to the Temple of Amun. His wife, Senay, was a Royal Nurse. Sennefer is presented wearing a long kilt, with his right hand placed on his knee, and his left arm around his wife. He wears a heavy wig, with elaborate jewellery, and his rolls of fat show his success in life. Senay wears a long dress and a heavy wig; her left hand is on her knee, and her right arm is around Sennefer. Their daughter, Mutnofret, stands between them, while on the left side of the statue another daughter, Nefertari, can be seen.

## 64. A Statue of Amenhotep Son of Hapu as a Young Man

*JE 44861; granite; H. 128cm; 18th Dynasty, New Kingdom; Karnak Temple, Luxor; Ground Floor, Room 12*
Amenhotep Son of Hapu was one of the most important officials from the reign of Amenhotep III; he was renowned throughout Egyptian history as an architect and a sage, and worshipped alongside Imhotep as a god of medicine. Amenhotep worked his way up the administration until he became the king's closest advisor, by this time he held the titles Royal Scribe and Overseer of the Works of the King. Many statues of Amenhotep have been found; in this particular example he is shown as a young scribe wearing a short wig, and sitting cross-legged in the typical scribal position – emphasising his learning. His papyrus scroll is unrolled on his legs, and his scribal equipment is over his shoulder. The rolls of fat on his stomach represent his success.

JE 90237

## 65. Scenes Representing the Country of Punt

*JE 14276; limestone; H. 49.3cm; 18th Dynasty, New Kingdom; Deir el-Bahri, Luxor; Ground Floor, Room 12*

Five scenes from Deir el-Bahri can be seen in the Egyptian Museum. These originally came from the southern part of the west wall of the Second level of Queen Hatshepsut's mortuary temple, and depict an expedition to the land of Punt in the 9th year of her reign. Missions had been sent to Punt since at least the 5th Dynasty, but here, for the first time, we see the landscape of Punt depicted. The Chief of Punt, Parehu, and his wife, Ati, are presented in a very detailed manner, with the Queen of Punt's unusual body shape strikingly shown. In other scenes, she is carried on a donkey, which the ancient Egyptians found humorous due to the lack of regality in this mode of transport. Behind them can be seen servants and followers bringing the products of Punt for the Egyptians.

## 66. A Statue of Amenhotep Son of Hapu as an Old Man

*JE 36368; granite; H. 117cm; 18th Dynasty, New Kingdom; Karnak Temple, Luxor; Ground Floor, Room 12*

This statue depicts Amenhotep as an old man with long hair, kneeling on a base. He wears a long kilt tied above the stomach. His age can be seen in his face, which is presented in a realistic manner.

## 67. A Statue of Amenhotep II

*JE 36680; schist; H. 57cm; 18th Dynasty, New Kingdom; Karnak Temple, Luxor; Ground Floor, Room 12*

Here Amenhotep II can be seen striding forward with his left leg, his arms extended down his sides, holding a folded cloth in each of his hands - a symbol of authority. He wears the royal nemes-headdress on his head, and a uraeus can be seen at his forehead. He has a short kilt, tied by a belt that has one of his cartouches at the centre, inscribed with the name Aakheperure. The king's face is carved in an idealistic manner: he has a long nose, with a beautifully carved mouth. The body is not as well carved as the face, showing that the sculptor wanted to place more emphasis on this area of the statue.

JE 14276

JE 38574-5

128

## 68. The Chapel of Hathor

*JE 38574-5; painted sandstone; H. 225cm; 18th Dynasty, New Kingdom; Deir el-Bahri, Luxor; Ground Floor, Room 12*

This small Hathor chapel was made by Tuthmosis III at Deir el-Bahri between the Temple of Hatshepsut and the Middle Kingdom Temple of Montuhotep II. The chapel is rectangular, with a vaulted ceiling decorated with stars. On the back wall is a scene of Tuthmosis III offering to the god Amun-Ra, who sits on a throne. At the front, on the left wall, Tuthmosis is accompanied by his wife, Meritre, before the divine cow and Hathor, while on the right wall Tuthmosis is shown with two princesses. Scenes on either side of the shrine, in the middle, show Tuthmosis III being suckled by the divine cow, followed by scenes of Tuthmosis and the goddess Hathor in human form.

The statue of Hathor as the divine cow, in the middle of the shrine, is inscribed for Amenhotep II, Tuthmosis III's son and successor. Hathor's head is surmounted by a uraeus, a solar-disc, and two short plumes. Amenhotep can be seen twice in the statue: once at the front beneath the cow's head, and a second time presented as a young boy nursing beneath the cow's right side.

## 69. A Statue of Senenmut with Neferure

*JE 37438; black granite; H. 60cm; 18th Dynasty, New Kingdom; Karnak Temple, Luxor; Ground Floor, Room 12*

Senenmut was an important noble during the reign of Hatshepsut, and some believe that he was the lover of the queen. He was in charge of her architectural projects, and responsible for making her royal tomb; he was also tutor to Hatshepsut's daughter, Neferure. Over twenty statues depicting Senenmut have been found, highlighting his importance. This particular piece shows him enveloped by a robe, embracing Princess Neferure beneath the garment so that only her head can be seen emerging; the accompanying inscriptions provide his titles associated with the palace and the Temple of Amun at Karnak. He is presented as a young man, with large eyes, and a smiling mouth. Neferure is shown in the conventional manner for children in ancient Egypt, a finger raised against her mouth, and shaven-headed except for a single thick lock of hair hanging to the right side of her head – known as the side-lock of youth. She has a royal uraeus at her forehead.

pages 128-129 | **68. The Chapel of Hathor** | *JE 38574-5; painted sandstone; H. 225cm; 18th Dynasty, New Kingdom; Deir el-Bahri, Luxor; Ground Floor, Room 12*
page 131 | **69. A Statue of Senenmut with Neferure** | *JE 37438; black granite; H. 60cm; 18th Dynasty, New Kingdom; Karnak Temple, Luxor; Ground Floor, Room 12*

130

## 70. The Stele of Ahmose I for Tetisheri

*JE 36335; limestone; H. 225cm; 18th Dynasty, New Kingdom; Abydos; Ground Floor, Room 12*

This stele was made in honour of King Ahmose's grandmother, Queen Tetisheri; in style it resembles the art of the Middle Kingdom. A winged sun-disc can be seen at the top of the stele, with a cobra hanging from either side. Below, King Ahmose stands offering to his grandmother, who sits before him. This scene is shown twice, one on the left of the stele, in which the king wears the White Crown, and the other on the right, in which he wears the Double Crown. Heaps of offerings can be seen before Tetisheri. The inscription below consists of seventeen lines, and describes how the king wanted to make a beautiful monument to Tetisheri's memory, and honour her temples.

## 71. A Seated Statue of Tuthmosis III

*JE 39260; granite; H. 169cm; 18th Dynasty, New Kingdom; Karnak Temple, Luxor; Ground Floor, Room 12*

This statue was originally found broken into three pieces. It presents Tuthmosis III wearing the nemes-headdress, with a uraeus at the forehead, and a large false beard attached to the chin. He is naked except for a short kilt, which is tied with an elaborate belt decorated with the royal cartouche. His left hand rests on his lap, while his right hand holds a piece of folded cloth – a symbol of authority. His feet each rest on the nine bows, representing the traditional enemies of Egypt.

## 72. A Statue of Amenhotep II with Meretseger

*JE 39394; granite; H. 125cm, 18th Dynasty, New Kingdom; Karnak Temple, Luxor; Ground Floor, Room 12*

This statue represents the king standing with his left leg striding forward, wearing the White Crown of Upper Egypt, and with a uraeus emerging from his forehead. Each foot stands on the image of the nine bows, which represent the combined enemies of Egypt. Both arms reach down and are held against his short kilt, which is decorated with a belt. His face is round, and he has large eyes. Behind Amenhotep is the goddess Meretseger, represented in the shape of a cobra. Her head is surmounted by a sun-disc and cow's horns. She is standing behind the king in order to protect him. On either side of the king are inscriptions providing his name and royal titles.

## 73. The Statue of Isis Mother of Tuthmosis III

*JE 37417; granite, with gold leaf on the crown; H. 98.5cm; Karnak Temple, Luxor; Ground Floor, Room 12*

Isis, mother of Tuthmosis III, was a secondary wife of Tuthmosis II. Here she is shown sitting on a throne with a base. Her hands are placed on her lap, but in her left hand she holds a lotus flower. She wears a large wig, with two cobras at the forehead; the left one wearing the White Crown of Upper Egypt and the right one wearing the Red Crown of Lower Egypt. She wears a wesekh-collar around her neck, and two large bracelets around her wrists. The base of a crown can be seen on top of her wig; it is covered in gold leaf and once held two large plumes. Her face is serene, and almost smiling. On either side of her legs are inscriptions, the one to her left introduces her as the king's mother.

133

**JE 39394**

**JE 39260**

134

## 74. A Standing Statue of Tuthmosis III

*JE 38234; schist; H. 2m; 18th Dynasty; New Kingdom; Karnak Temple, Luxor; Ground Floor, Room 12*

The king can be seen here standing in the conventional pose, wearing a kilt tied with a belt in which the royal cartouche can be seen. He wears the White Crown of Upper Egypt, with a uraeus at his forehead. His face is young, with almond eyes, a large nose, and a finely carved mouth, which bears a slight smile. His body is strong and idealistic, with his arms close by his sides, each hand gripping a folded cloth. His left leg can be seen striding forward, while his feet stand upon the nine bows, which represent the enemies of Egypt. The hieroglyphic inscription on the base refers to Akh-Menu (festival hall) at Karnak Temple - an area of the temple built under Tuthmosis III.

## 75. A Statue of Tuthmosis III Offering nw-Vessels

*JE 43507; Egyptian alabaster; H. 27.5cm; 18th Dynasty, New Kingdom; Deir el Medina, Luxor; Ground Floor, Room 12*

Tuthmosis III is one of the most important kings in Egyptian history; he led seventeen military campaigns into the Levant during his reign, leading to him being dubbed the Napoleon of ancient Egypt. Here we see him presented in a worshipful attitude, kneeling on a rectangular base, his hands resting on his knees and holding offering jars. He wears the royal nemes-headdress, with a uraeus cobra at his forehead. His face is detailed yet idealistic, and his expression is serene. He wears a short pleated kilt.

## 76. The Head of Amenhotep III

*JE 38597; clay, painted plaster; H. 38cm; 18th Dynasty, New Kingdom; Karnak Temple, Luxor; Ground Floor, Room 12*

This clay head shows Amenhotep III with the face of a young man, almost in the Amarna style, with large almond-shaped eyes. Consequently, this head can be dated to the end of his reign. He wears the Blue War Crown, decorated with many small circles, while a uraeus can be seen at the forehead.

## 77. A Sphinx of Queen Hatshepsut

*JE 53114; granite; L. 260cm; 18th Dynasty, New Kingdom; Deir el-Bahri, Luxor; Ground Floor, Room 6*

Hatshepsut is presented here in the form of a sphinx, in a similar manner to the Middle Kingdom sphinxes of Amenemhat III on display nearby. She has a human face with feminine features, displaying her power and dignity, and wears the nemes-headdress, a prominent false beard, and an elaborate collar composed of five rows of beads, followed by a row of tear-shaped pendants. Her front legs are extended before her, and her tail is wrapped around her rear right leg. Inscriptions provide her name and describe her as beloved of the god Amun.

JE 38234

137

138

JE 38597

JE 43507

139

# The Amarna Rooms
## A Brief History of the Amarna Period (c. 1352 - 1323 BC)

*One of the most exciting collections in the Egyptian Museum can be found in the Amarna room. Here you can see evidence relating to the life and beliefs of Akhenaten, the first recorded monotheist in history, who worshipped the sun-disc known as the Aten. Akhenaten started his reign as Amenhotep IV, and changed his name after his religious revolution began. We know that the changes in religion did not happen suddenly, and that they were not entirely a product of Akhenaten's time; already under his grandfather, Tuthmosis IV, there had been a move towards the supreme importance of the sun cult. Under Akhenaten, however, the name of the god Amun was forcibly removed from the temples; and later he would even go as far as closing the temples completely. There is even evidence that his followers smashed the name of Amenhotep III, Akhenaten's father, wherever they found it, simply because the word 'Amun' formed part of it. Later, they would also remove any reference to the word 'gods' because it is plural. Akhenaten worshipped the Aten in a new city, founded in Middle Egypt, called Akhetaten (modern Tell el-Amarna), which means Horizon of the Aten.*

*As well as creating a revolution in religion and architecture, Akhenaten also made one in art. The artists of this period developed a freer art style, so, for the first time, we see the king sitting with his family, eating and playing. Many scholars have also studied the statues of Akhenaten; these statues, many from Karnak and Tell el-Amarna, take a strange shape when compared to traditional Egyptian statuary. The king's body has a feminine style, with exaggerated eyes and mouth, and a large flabby stomach. Many people have argued that Akhenaten's art style was the result of the king having deformities, but, in my opinion, if you look at the poems written by Akhenaten, they explain that the Aten was seen as a combination of male and female aspects. This is what the artists of Akhetaten tried to bring to their statuary.*

*Hall 8*

## 78. A Relief Showing Akhenaten and his Family

*TR 10.11.26.4; painted limestone; H. 53cm; 18th Dynasty, New Kingdom; Tell el-Amarna; Ground Floor, Hall 8*

This relief was discovered within the royal tomb at Tell el-Amarna; it depicts the king and queen offering lotus flowers to the god Aten. The Aten itself is shown as a sun-disc, its rays ending with human hands providing life and prosperity. Behind the king and queen, their eldest daughter, Meritaten can be seen holding a sistrum with one hand, and holding the hand of her younger sister Meketaten with the other. The two are depicted wearing long transparent dresses, in the typical style of the Amarna Period. Each figure has thick lips, flabby stomachs, large ears, and narrow eyes. Nefertiti is wearing a long wig and a crown with a uraeus, surmounted by two horns, a sun-disc, and two long plumes. There is a clear similarity between the faces of Akhenaten and his family. The scene is accompanied by prayers to the Aten, and the titles and names of each member of the royal family.

page 141 | **78. A Relief Showing Akhenaten and his Family** | *TR 10.11.26.4; painted limestone; H. 53cm; 18th Dynasty, New Kingdom; Tell el-Amarna; Ground Floor, Hall 8*

140

141

## 79. A Statue of Akhenaten with a Female Figure

*JE 44866; limestone; H. 39.5cm; 18th Dynasty, New Kingdom; Tell el-Amarna; Ground Floor, Hall 8*

This unfinished seated statue of Akhenaten illustrates well the unusual features of art in this period. The king is depicted sitting on a throne, wearing the Blue Crown, with the royal uraeus at his forehead. The female figure, sitting on his lap, is thought to be his daughter Meritaten; however, it is also possible that the female figure is Akhenaten's second wife, Kiya, as it was conventional for children to be depicted with a side-lock of youth, whereas here the female figure wears a wig, typical of an adult.

Akhenaten is shown with his right hand on the female figure's chest, while she touches his elbow. It was not normal in Egyptian art to show such a close relationship between the king and his children, if indeed this is what is depicted here, but after Akhenaten's religious revolution such subjects began to be shown for the first time, including scenes of the royal family enjoying themselves in the palace.

## 80. A Statue of Akhenaten Presenting an Offering

*JE 43580; limestone; H. 35cm; 18th Dynasty, New Kingdom; Tell el-Amarna; Ground Floor, Hall 8*

This statue presents the king standing wearing the Blue Crown and a finely carved short kilt, holding an offering table out for the Aten with his two hands. The king's body and face show strong features, and are presented in a weaker form of the Amarna style. Although it was traditional for kings to be shown with their left leg striding forward, here Akhenaten's feet are held close together. A hole can be seen in the crown, originally for a royal uraeus. A plinth rises from the base along the king's back, adding support to the statue.

page 143 | **79. A Statue of Akhenaten with a Female Figure** | *JE 44866; limestone; H. 39.5cm; 18th Dynasty, New Kingdom; Tell el-Amarna; Ground Floor, Hall 8*
pages 144-145 | **80. A Statue of Akhenaten Presenting an Offering** | *JE 43580; limestone; H. 35cm; 18th Dynasty, New Kingdom; Tell el-Amarna; Ground Floor, Hall 8*

JE 43580

## 81. A Canopic Jar, possibly for Kiya, Secondary Wife of Akhenaten

*JE 39637; Egyptian alabaster; H. 38cm; 18th Dynasty, New Kingdom; Valley of the Kings, Luxor; Ground Floor, Room 3*

Many objects belonging to Queen Tiye, Kiya, Akhenaten and Amenhotep III were found in the mysterious Tomb KV 55 in the Valley of the Kings. It has been argued that this tomb was used as a burial place for remains and objects brought to Thebes from Tell el-Amarna after Akhenaten's death. This canopic jar is one of four found in the tomb; it is possible that it was originally made for Meritaten, Akhenaten's daughter, who may have married the enigmatic King Smenkhkare, though many now assign it to Kiya, or even Smenkhkare himself.

## 82. A Colossal Statue of Akhenaten

*JE 49529; sandstone; H. 293cm; 18th Dynasty, New Kingdom; Temple of Aten, Karnak Temple, Luxor; Ground Floor, Room 3*

A group of colossal statues of Akhenaten, originally from the Temple of the Aten at Karnak, are on display in the Egyptian Museum. These statues may represent the first time that Akhenaten's new religious thoughts were translated into art and architecture. Here we see the king standing, wearing a kilt that hangs below his swollen stomach. It is tied with a belt, decorated with the royal cartouche. He wears the Double Crown of Upper and Lower Egypt, as well as the Khat-headdress. In his hands he holds symbols of power and authority. His features are presented in the typical style of the period, with narrow slanting eyes, a long thin face, and thick lips.

## 83. The Coffin of Akhenaten

*JE 39626; gilded wood; L. 185cm; 18th Dynasty, New Kingdom; Valley of the Kings, Luxor; Ground Floor, Room 3*

This coffin was discovered in tomb KV 55, in the Valley of the Kings, in 1907 by Theodore Davis. Within, Davis found a skeleton that scholars initially attributed to Queen Tiye, wife of Amenhotep III. However, after further careful examination, they found that it was the body of a king, rather than that of a queen. It was then argued that because the body appeared to be that of a twenty-five year old male, it could be King Smenkhkare; however, the British Egyptologist Alan Gardiner, who studied the coffin, found many epithets that connected it with Akhenaten.

The lower part of the coffin was stolen during restoration work and was missing from 1915-1931. It was found again in 1972 and put on display in Munich in an exhibition called the Secrets of the Golden Coffin. In 2002 the museum returned the coffin to Cairo.

JE 39637

147

JE 49529

## 84. The Unfinished Head of Nefertiti

*JE 95286; quartzite; H. 35.5.cm; 18th Dynasty, New Kingdom; Tell el-Amarna; Ground Floor, Room 3*

This head was carved as part of a composite statue - a statue that consists of many parts, each being made separately. Despite being incomplete, it is one of the most beautiful sculptures known from ancient Egypt, even more so, in my opinion, than the bust of Nefertiti in Berlin. The carving is typical of the Amarna Period: the long eyebrows are in keeping with the thin mouth, with its faint smile, and the unfinished eyes give the piece an aura of magic and mystery. A crown was originally fitted on top of the head. Lines betray the unfinished nature of the piece, and provide us with details about the artist's working practices.

## 85. A Second Colossal Statue of Akhenaten

*JE 49528; sandstone; H. 170cm (upper part only); 18th Dynasty, New Kingdom; Temple of Aten, Karnak Temple, Luxor; Ground Floor, Room 3*

This statue, one of the colossal statues that originally stood in front of the pillared hall of the Temple of the Aten at Karnak, presents the king wearing the royal nemes-headdress with a uraeus at the forehead, surmounted by two ostrich plumes, symbol of Shu, the god of air. The king stands in an osiride style, holding the royal symbols of power and authority in his hands, crossed at his chest. The artistic style is conventional for the period, with exaggerated eyes and lips, and a long face ending in a false beard.

## 86. A Relief of Akhenaten and his Family Offering to the Aten

*TR 30.10.26.12; limestone; H. 102cm; 18th Dynasty, New Kingdom; Tell el-Amarna; Ground Floor, Room 3*

This stele was found in the Great Palace of Akhenaten at Tell el-Amarna. It shows the Aten at the top right, its rays raining down upon the royal family, ending with human hands, which in some cases hold the ankh-sign of life. The king stands closest to the Aten, presented in the typical Amarna style, wearing the White Crown of Upper Egypt, with a uraeus at the forehead. He wears a kilt that extends to his knees. Behind, the queen wears a headdress and a tight dress, while behind her, the young Princess Meritaten can be seen. All three figures are presented in the act of offering.

TR 30.10.26.12

151

JE 95286

152

JE 49528

# The New Kingdom Continued

## 87. The Statues of Amun and Mut

*JE 99064; limestone; H. 414cm; 18th Dynasty, New Kingdom; Karnak Temple, Luxor; Ground Floor, Hall 8*

These statues have undergone extensive restoration work; the head of the goddess was originally excavated by Auguste Mariette at Karnak in 1873, with further parts being found over the course of many years in subsequent excavations. They present the gods Amun and Mut, seated on large thrones. Mut places her right hand on her knee, and the other on her husband. She wears a tight dress, beautifully decorated with two straps over her shoulders. On her head she wears three styles of wig, which are surmounted by the Double Crown.

The god Amun can be seen with his right hand on his knee, and his left hand holding the ankh-sign of life. His throne is decorated on both sides with the symbols of the unification of the Two Lands – the sema tawy. The throne is inscribed with the names of the gods, and, beside Amun, we can see his name and title: Amun-Ra, Lord of the Thrones of the Two Lands, who lives in Karnak. Beside Mut, we can see the title Lady of Isheru, which is a site in Karnak. The base of the statue is inscribed for King Horemheb, who is described as beloved of Mut and Amun.

## 88. The Saqqara Tablet

*JE 11335; limestone; H. 160cm; 19th Dynasty, New Kingdom; Saqqara; Ground Floor, Hall 9*

This is a very important historical piece in the museum, which I believe everyone should see, as it helps us to reconstruct the order of the kings of Egypt. The tablet originally listed the names of the pharaohs from King Anedjib of the 1st Dynasty to Ramesses II of the 19th Dynasty; today forty-seven royal cartouches are still preserved on the piece. It is of similar importance to the Palermo Stone, the Turin papyri, and the Karnak and Abydos kings-lists as a source for the study of Egyptian history.

page 155 | **87. The Statues of Amun and Mut** | *JE 99064; limestone; H. 414cm; 18th Dynasty, New Kingdom; Karnak Temple, Luxor; Ground Floor, Hall 8*
pages 156-157 | **88. The Saqqara Tablet** | *JE 11335(a); limestone; H. 160cm; 19th Dynasty, New Kingdom; Saqqara; Ground Floor, Hall 9*

JE 11335

## 89. The Statue of Ramesses II as a Child with the God Hauron
*JE 64735; granite, limestone; H. 231cm; 19th Dynasty, New Kingdom; Tanis; Ground Floor, Hall 10*

This is one of the most beautiful statues in the museum. It represents Ramesses II as a child, sitting in front of the Levantine sun god Hauron, who is in the shape of a hawk. Ramesses is presented in the typical manner for an Egyptian child: naked, his finger to his mouth, with a large side-lock of youth hanging from the right side of his head. He also has a uraeus at his forehead, and a sun-disc above his head. He holds the sw-plant in his left hand. It has been argued that the statue can be read to spell out the name of the king: the sun-disc represents *Ra*, the child is *mes*, and the *sw* plant is the final element – *Ra-mes-sw*. The limestone face of the hawk was found in a separate location from the rest of the piece.

## 90. A Statue of Meritamun
*JE 31413; limestone; H. 75cm; 19th Dynasty, New Kingdom; Ramesseum, Luxor; Ground Floor, Hall 15*

Despite the fact that only the titles of the queen are visible, it is known that this is a statue of Meritamun, a daughter and consort of Ramesses II, due to an almost identical piece being found in Akhmim. It is remarkable due to its beautiful colour, and the detail of the tripartite wig. Meritamun wears a uraeus at her forehead, while a diadem of cobras, each with a sun-disc, surmounts her wig. She also wears a large pectoral around her neck, and a tight fitting dress. She holds a menat-necklace in her left hand, which was shaken during religious ceremonies.

## 91. A Bust of Ramesses II
*CG 616; granite; H. 80cm; 19th Dynasty, New Kingdom; Tanis; Ground Floor, Room 14*

This bust of Ramesses II closely resembles a statue of Ramesses in the Turin Egyptian Museum, Italy. However, the Cairo piece wears a long wig, rather than the blue crown worn by the Turin statue. A uraeus can be seen at the king's forehead, and he is shown with a young face, and a slight smile. His nose is missing. Below, he wears a collar composed of five rows of beads, and a tight pleated robe.

page 159 | **89. The Statue of Ramesses II as a Child with the God Hauron** | *JE 64735; granite, limestone; H. 231cm; 19th Dynasty, New Kingdom; Tanis; Ground Floor, Hall 10*
page 160 | **90. A Statue of Meritamun** | *JE 31413; limestone; H. 75cm; 19th Dynasty, New Kingdom; Ramesseum, Luxor; Ground Floor, Hall 15*
page 161 | **91. A Bust of Ramesses II** | *CG 616; granite; H. 80cm; 19th Dynasty, New Kingdom; Tanis; Ground Floor, Room 14*

JE 31413

160

CG 616

# The Monuments of the Later Periods

*A Brief History of the Later Periods (Third Intermediate Period, c. 1069 – 664 BC; Late Period, 664 – 332 BC; Ptolemaic Period, 332 – 30 BC; Roman Period, 30 BC - 395 AD)*

*Following the New Kingdom centralised power was lost in Egypt again, with power in the North divided between a number of powerful local rulers, while in the south the High Priests of Amun ruled from Karnak. This is known as the Third Intermediate Period. Unity was achieved again with the 25th Dynasty, but not for long, as Egypt was subject to a series of Persian invasions, followed by the coming of Alexander the Great and the Ptolemaic Period. With the death of Cleopatra VII, Egypt became part of the Roman Empire.*

*Hall 25*

## 92. The Head of King Shabaka

*JE 36677; granite; H. 97cm; 25th Dynasty, Third Intermediate Period; Karnak Temple, Luxor; Ground Floor, Hall 25*

Only the head of Shabaka is on display here, although it will originally have formed part of a colossal statue of the king. He wears the Double Crown of Upper and Lower Egypt above his nemes-headdress, and two uraei can be seen at his forehead. This latter element is typical of the 25th Dynasty.

page 163 | **92.The Head of King Shabaka** | *JE 36677; granite; H. 97cm; 25th Dynasty, Third Intermediate Period; Karnak Temple, Luxor; Ground Floor, Hall 25*

162

## 93. A Statue of Osiris

*CG 38358; schist; H. 89.5cm; 26th Dynasty, Late Period; Saqqara; Ground Floor, Room 24*

This beautiful statue was discovered in a deep pit in the tomb of Psammtik at Saqqara. Osiris is shown seated, wrapped tightly, and holding the crook and flail - symbols of kingship – in his hands, crossed at his torso. He wears the atef-crown and a uraeus, as well as a false beard. The base is inscribed with a conventional offering formula.

## 94. A Statue of Hathor and Psammtik

*CG 784; schist; H. 96cm; 26th Dynasty; Late Period; Saqqara; Ground Floor, Room 24*

This statue depicts the important official Psammtik with the goddess Hathor in the form of a divine cow. The cow's body has been expertly carved, with the details of her muscles being very clear. Hathor wears a thin collar around her neck, and a solar disc with a uraeus, surmounted by double plumes, on her head. Psammtik stands below Hathor's head, protected by her. He wears a wig and a necklace, and holds his arms down along his kilt, which is inscribed with hieroglyphic texts, in an attitude of prayer.

## 95. A Statue of the Goddess Isis

*CG 38884; schist; H. 90cm; 26th Dynasty, Late Period; Saqqara; Ground Floor, Room 24*

This statue was found in the tomb of the Chief of Scribes, Overseer of the Seal, and Governor of the Palace, Psammtik, at Saqqara. It represents Isis, the mother of Horus, in the form of a beautiful woman. She is seated, wearing a long tight dress, her left hand is placed on her knee, while her right hand holds the ankh-symbol of life. Isis is often associated with Hathor, and here is presented wearing the latter goddess' crown – the cow's horns surmounted by a sun-disc. The base of the statue bears an inscription dedicating the statue to Isis from Psammtik.

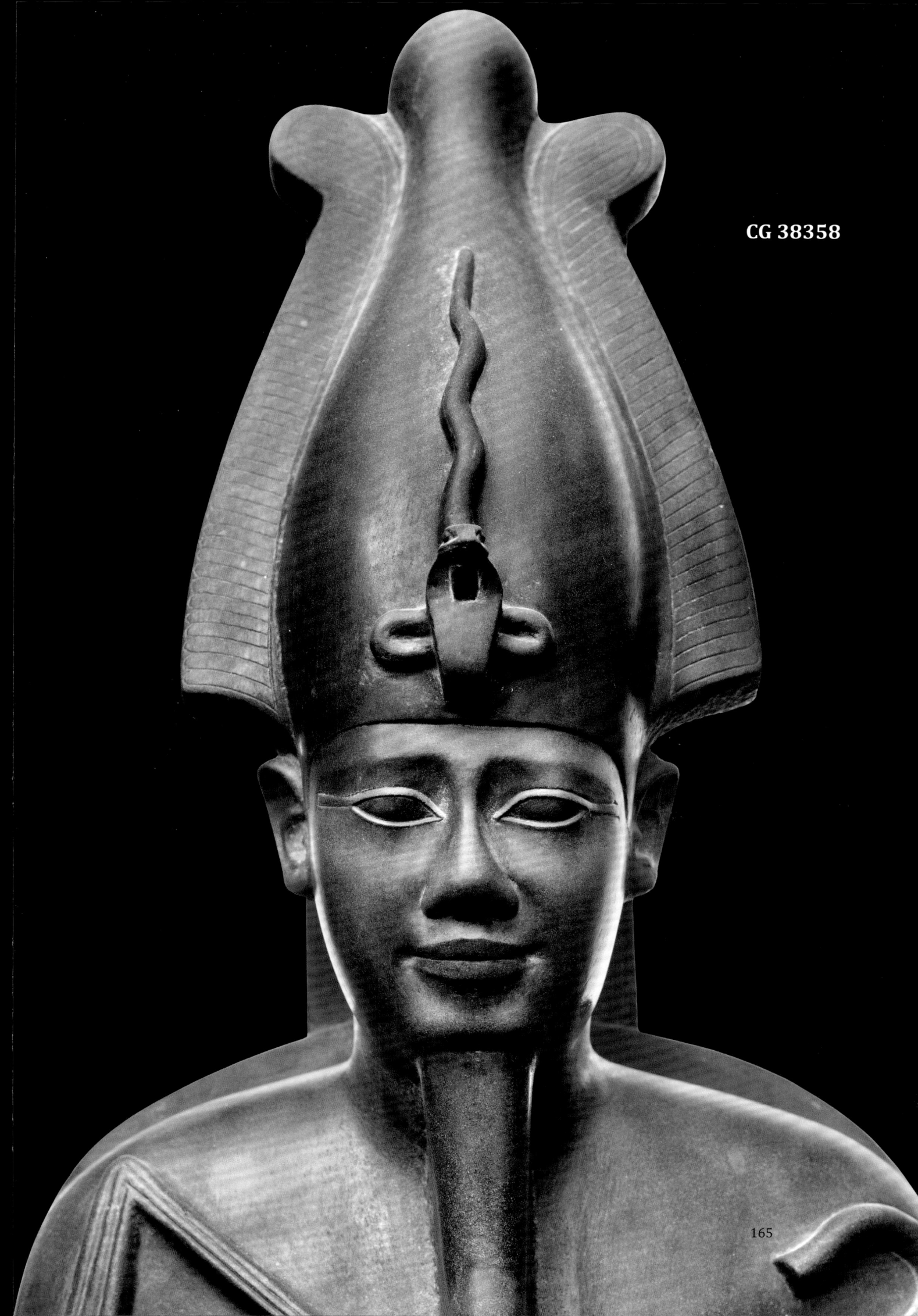

165

CG 784

CG 38884

## 96. The Statue of Montuemhat

*JE 36993; granite; H. 137cm; 25th-26th Dynasty, Late Period; Karnak Temple, Luxor; Ground Floor, Room 24*

Montuemhat was a member of a family of priests of Amun and Montu based at Thebes. He held the titles Fourth Priest of Amun, Mayor of Thebes and Governor of Upper Egypt, and lived between the 25th and 26th Dynasties. Many inscriptions and statues are known for this man, highlighting his importance during this tumultuous period. This particular statue was found in two pieces, but has since been restored. Montuemhat stands in a conventional manner, his left leg striding forward, and his arms placed firmly against his sides. His fists are clenched, each holding a folded cloth – a symbol of authority. He wears a short kilt, tied with a belt inscribed with his name and titles, and a wide heavy wig on his head.

*Hall 30*

## 97. A Statue of Amunirdis the Elder

*JE 3420; alabaster with a granite base; H. 170cm; 25th Dynasty, Third Intermediate Period; Karnak Temple, Luxor; Ground Floor, Hall 30*

This is one of the most celebrated statues of Amunirdis the Elder, daughter of King Kashta of the 25th Dynasty. It was discovered by Auguste Mariette within a small chapel at Karnak Temple. She is presented wearing a diadem of cobras on top of her wig, with a further two cobras and a vulture at her forehead. She wears a long tight dress, and holds a necklace in her right hand and a flagellum in her left.

page 169 | **96. The Statue of Montuemhat** | *JE 36993; granite; H. 137cm; 25th-26th Dynasty, Late Period; Karnak Temple, Luxor; Ground Floor, Room 24*
page 170 | **97. A Statue of Amunirdis the Elder** | *JE 3420; alabaster with a granite base; H. 170cm; 25th Dynasty, Third Intermediate Period; Karnak Temple, Luxor; Ground Floor, Hall 30*

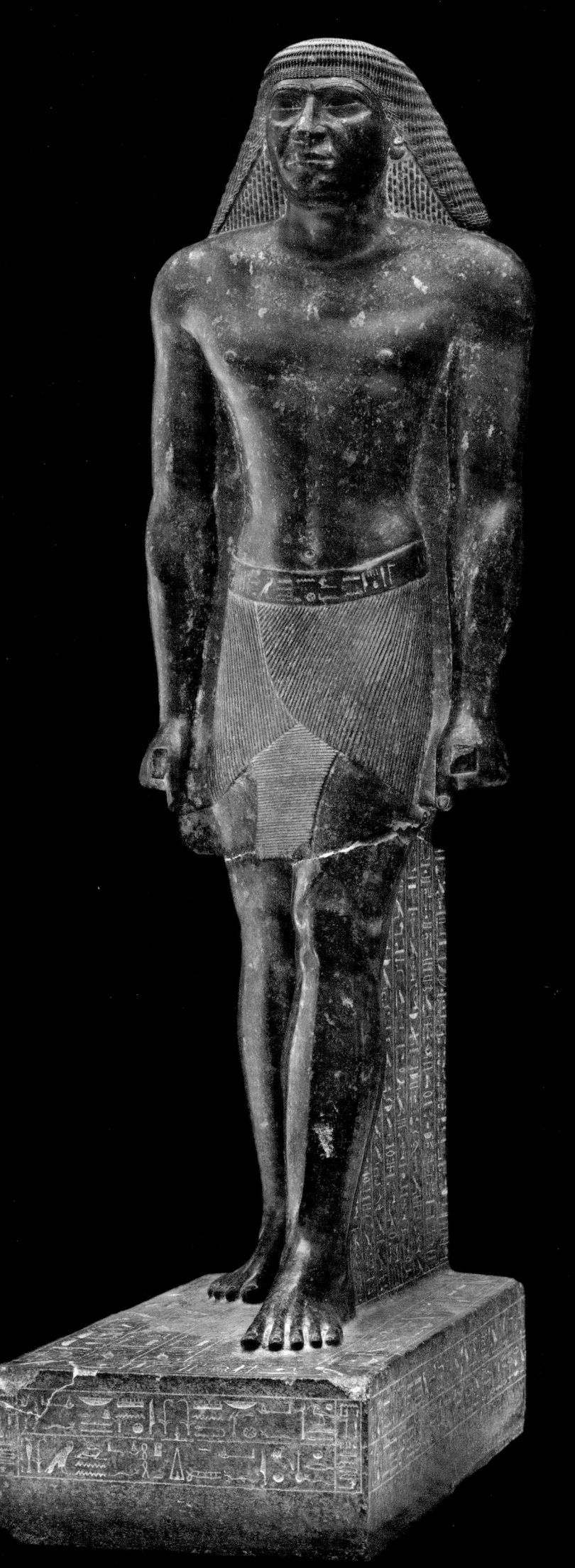

170

## 98. A Stele dedicated by Ptolemy V to the Buchis Bull

*JE 54313; painted limestone; H. 72cm; Ptolemaic Period; Armant;  Ground Floor, Room 34*

This stele depicts King Ptolemy V making an offering to the Buchis Bull. At the top of the stele can be seen a winged sun-disc, while below can be seen two recumbent jackals, seated either side of two rearing uraei. A djed-pillar of stability is between them, and a scarab above. Below is the main register of the stele: the Buchis bull stands on the left, above a platform; it wears two uraei, a sun-disc and two plumes. Behind, he is protected by the god Montu in the form of a hawk. Ptolemy stands to the right offering the hieroglyphic symbol for fields. Below are five rows of hieroglyphs running horizontally, describing the birth and life of the sacred bull. The Buchis bull was associated with the God Montu, and buried in the Bucheum at the site of Armant near Luxor.

## 99. The Coffin of Petosiris

*JE 46592; wood, coloured glass; L. 175cm; Ptolemaic Period; Tuna el-Gebel, Ashmunein; Ground Floor, Hall 49*

This wooden coffin belongs to the early Ptolemaic Period High Priest of Thoth, Petosiris, who was buried in Tuna el-Gebel in Middle Egypt, within a family tomb that resembles a Ptolemaic Temple. Petosiris wears a wig, a false beard, and has inlaid eyes. Five vertical columns of hieroglyphics, formed from coloured glass inlays, can be seen down the middle of the coffin; these display the name and titles of Petosiris, and also Chapter 42 of the Book of the Dead. The hieroglyphs are surmounted by a row of stars.

page 171 | **98. A Stele dedicated by Ptolemy V to the Buchis Bull** | *JE 54313; painted limestone; H. 72cm; Ptolemaic Period; Armant;  Ground Floor, Room 34*
page 173 | **99. The Coffin of Petosiris** | *JE 46592; wood, coloured glass; L. 175cm; Ptolemaic Period; Tuna el-Gebel, Ashmunein; Ground Floor, Hall 49*

JE 46592

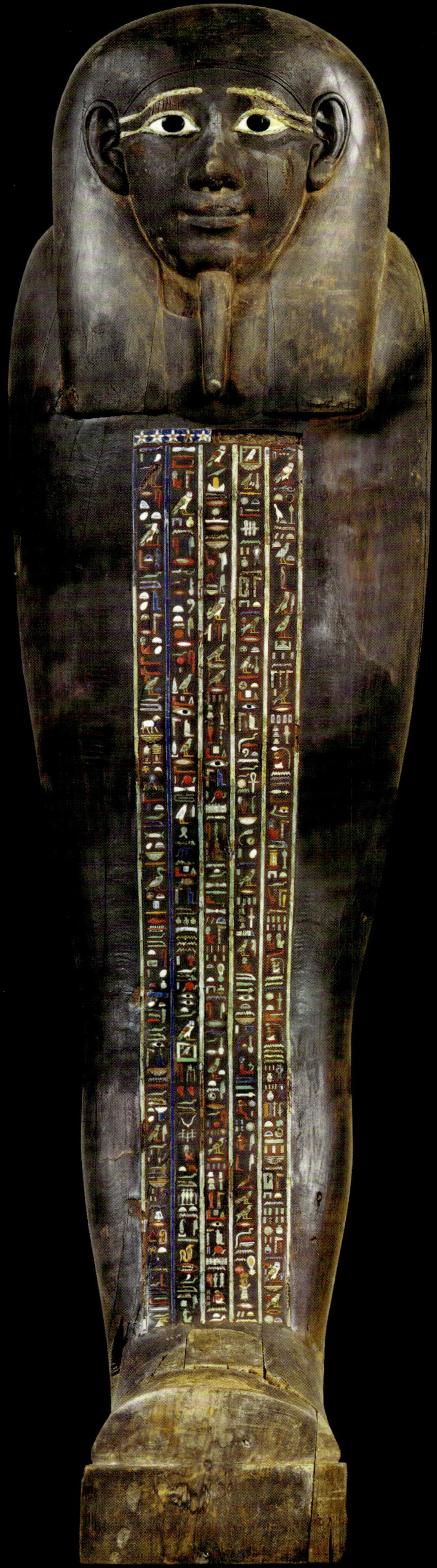

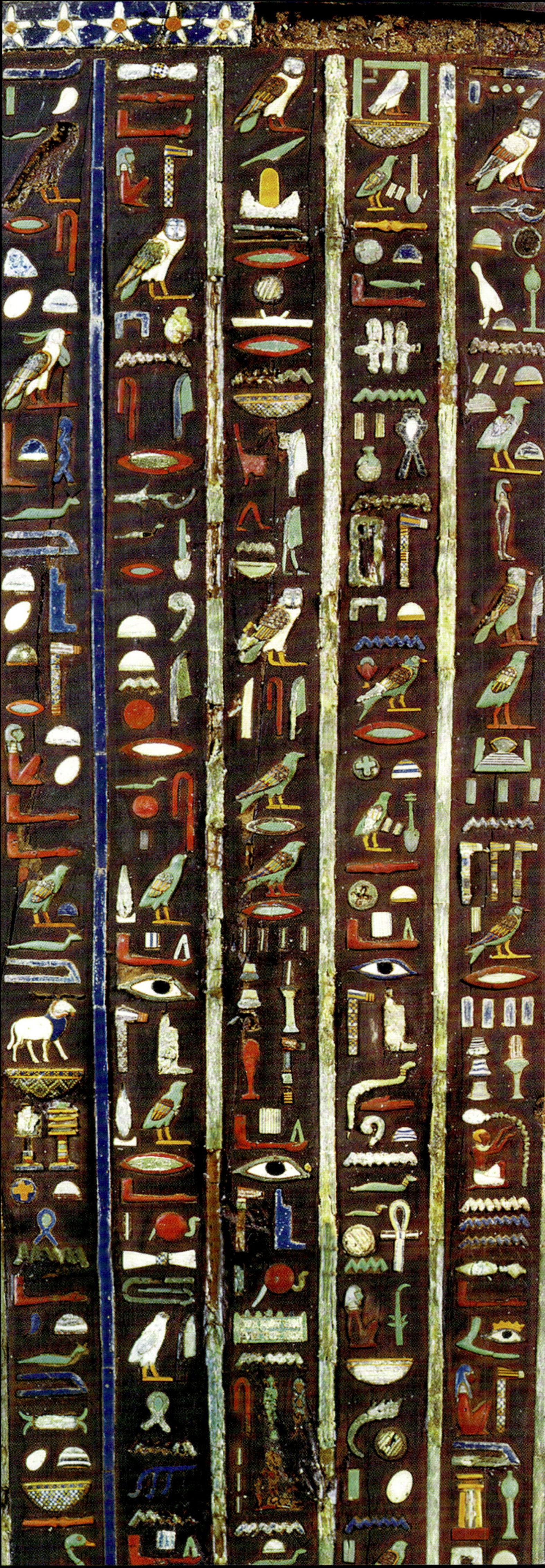

# IV
# The Upper Floor of the Museum

Our tour of the upper floor of the Egyptian Museum begins at the top of the staircase on the south-eastern side of the building.

## A Brief History of the Royal Mummies

*There are two mummy rooms in the Egyptian Museum: one room contains the royal mummies of the late Second Intermediate Period and Early New Kingdom kings and queens, such as Seqenenre Tao, Amenhotep I, Meritamun, Tuthmosis I, Tuthmosis II, Tuthmosis III, Amenhotep II, Tuthmosis IV, Seti I, Ramesses II, Merenptah, Seti II, and the mummy of Hatshepsut; while the second room, located on the west side of the museum, contains the mummies of the later New Kingdom and the Third Intermediate Period, such as Ramesses III, Ramesses IV, Ramesses V, Ramesses VI, Ramesses IX, Pinudjem II, Istemkheb D, Maatkare, Nodjmet, Henuttawy, and Khonsuemhat.*

*Mummification was practiced in Egypt from the beginning of Egyptian history; it is even evidenced in the Predynastic Period. Once, when I was excavating a 2nd Dynasty tomb at Saqqara, located to the south of the burials of the officials of the 1st Dynasty, I found a sealed wooden coffin. There was a skeleton inside and, after careful study, it was clear that there had been an attempt to mummify the lower parts. Other early mummy remains were found under the Step Pyramid of Djoser at Saqqara, while another royal mummy, whose identity has not been firmly established, is on display in the Imhotep Museum, Saqqara. The mummy of Nefer, also of Old Kingdom date, is another impressive example of early mummification attempts.*

*Over time mummification techniques became more sophisticated. In the New Kingdom it was normal for the body to be dried in natron for seventy days, and for the internal organs, as well as the brain, to be removed. The body would be packed and wrapped with linen, and covered in resins, to help preserve its shape and to stop decomposition. The heart would be left inside the body, however, as it was necessary to enter the afterlife.*

*In the first hall we see eleven mummies who have recently been placed within new cases to help control humidity and heat. Such conservation methods are important because mummies cannot be restored, they need to be preserved. Currently, to enhance their protection even further, we are undertaking an important project with the Getty Conservation Institute, designing new special cases for the royal mummies.*

*In two years the National Museum of Egyptian Civilisation will be opened in Fustat. At this time the mummies of the kings will be moved to this new location, and displayed in a different manner from that of the Egyptian Museum. I do not like to display mummies for a thrill, I like to present them for education; therefore, I believe it is important that people are not able to see their faces. Instead, visitors will have the ability to learn about the mummification process, the Egyptians' afterlife beliefs, and the events of each king's life through computer graphics and photographs. The CT-scan results for each mummy will be on display, so that visitors can discover how and when they died, while in another hall we will present the results of our DNA studies. At the time of writing, we have so far identified the members of the family of King Tutankhamun, and almost completely* identified and examined all the mummies of the 18th Dynasty. This year we began a study of the Ramesside royal family, in which we intend to focus on the following: first, the correct identification of each mummy, because some may have been misidentified or placed in the wrong coffin when moved in antiquity; and secondly, we will be able to discover the exact relationship between the so-called mummy of Ramesses I, currently in Luxor Museum, and the mummy of his son Seti I, or his grandson Ramesses II.

The mummies that you see in the Egyptian Museum were discovered in three major cachettes. The first one was found south of Deir el-Bahri, Luxor, in 1881, in tomb 320. The story is very exciting and has been repeated many times: In 1875, a member of the Abdul Rassul family was leading his goats at Deir el-Bahri. At one point, while chasing after one of the goats, he looked inside the cliff and found a shaft. He was able to climb carefully into this shaft and, after descending, found himself standing in front of a treasure of gold and coffins. The family kept their discovery secret, and only returned there three times over the course of ten years. Then, Maspero discovered that mummies and royal objects were being sold in Europe, and so he sent a team of archaeologists, including Ahmed Pasha Kamal, to Luxor. After their arrival, one man from the Abdul Rassul family was arrested and taken to prison, but he would not tell anyone about their discovery. After his release, he told his family about all the suffering that he had undergone and asked them for a greater share of the money; this started a fight, after which one member of the family went to the police and the entire story came out.

The Egyptian government began to move all forty mummies to Cairo in 1881. When the mummies arrived at the port at Bulaq the customs official looked in his categories of goods for the word 'mummy,' but could not find it, and so did not know how to document the cargo, so he refused to allow them to enter Cairo. Then, however, after some thought, he found the entry for 'salted fish,' and so let them enter under this heading!

This cachette contained the mummies of many of the great kings of Egypt, such as Seqenenre Tao, Ahmose, Amenhotep I, Tuthmosis I, Tuthmosis II, Tuthmosis III, Seti I, Ramesses II, Ramesses III, Ramesses IX, Pinudjem II, and another seven mummies of the queens of Dynasties 18 – 21, such as Ahmose-Nefertari, wife of Ahmose, Sitkamose, probably a daughter of Kamose, Nodjmet, queen of Herihor, Maatkare, queen of Osorkon I, Istemkheb, daughter of the High Priest of Amun Menkheperre, and Nesikhonsu, wife of Pinudjem II.

The second cachette was found by Victor Loret in 1898, behind a decorated wall in the tomb of Amenhotep II, whose mummy was found in his own sarcophagus. It contained twelve mummies, of which nine (including Amenhotep II) were moved by Howard Carter to the Egyptian Museum when he was chief inspector of the west bank of Luxor. After cutting a hole in the wall Loret discovered the mummies of Tuthmosis IV, Amenhotep III, Merenptah, Seti II, Siptah, Ramesses IV, Ramesses V, Ramesses VI, and three unidentified women and a boy. During our project to identify the family of King Tutankhamun through DNA analysis we found that the elder unidentified Lady from the tomb is Queen Tiye, the famous wife of Amenhotep III, while the younger lady, who was once identified by an English Egyptologist as Nefertiti, is the mother of Tutankhamun. However, we still do not know her name, and so cannot state for certain which queen she was.

The third most important cachette at Deir el-Bahri was again found by the Abdul Rassul family, and has been dubbed the cache of the priests. Mohammed Abdul Rassul led the antiquities Director, Hermann Grapow, to the entrance of a shaft near the tomb of Queen Neferu at Deir el-Bahri. After 8m they found an entrance on the north wall to a room closed with leaves, the remains of wood, and pieces of stone. After reaching the bottom of the shaft they found a narrow tunnel on the south wall, cut into the rock slope, full of wooden coffins. After inspection these were found to date to the 21st Dynasty, and belonged to the priests of Amun. More tunnels and rooms were found as the excavation work continued. The Antiquities Department began to move these coffins on November 5th 1891, and as they cleared they found that there were one hundred and fifty-three coffins inside, but the mummies within had all been plundered. These coffins were moved to the Egyptian Museum in May 1892, and were not displayed until the winter of 1892.

# The First Mummy Room *(Upper Floor, Room 56)*

*The first mummy room in the Egyptian Museum can be found on the south-eastern side of the museum at the top of the staircase.*

## 100. The Mummy of Seqenenre Tao

*CG 61051; 170cm; 17th Dynasty, Second Intermediate Period; Deir el-Bahri, Luxor; Upper Floor, Room 56*

Seqenenre was a Theban king of the 17th Dynasty. He began the struggle against the Hyksos - foreign rulers who controlled the Delta during the Second Intermediate Period for more than 100 years. It is thought that he was killed in a battle against them, at about the age of forty, evidenced by wounds clearly visible in his skull. A later Ramesside tale relates how Seqenenre received a letter from the Hyksos ruler in the north, telling him that the noise of the Theban hippopotami was keeping him awake in the Delta. The aim was probably to show that although there was a great distance between them, the Hyksos were still causing the Thebans problems. Seqenenre's son, Kamose, would continue the war against the Hyksos.

## 101. The Mummy of Amenhotep I

*JE 26211; L. 165cm; 18th Dynasty, New Kingdom; Deir el-Bahri, Luxor; Upper Floor, Room, 56*

The son of King Ahmose, Amenhotep I ruled for 21 years. His tomb has not yet been found, although many scholars are currently searching for it; some believe that it is located behind the temple of Hatshepsut at Deir el-Bahri, whereas others, such as Daniel Polz of the German Institute, believe that the tomb is in Dra Abu el-Naga. Amenhotep's mummy has never been unwrapped, and is still covered with ancient flowers.

## 102. The Mummy of Tuthmosis II

*JE 26212; L. 168.5cm; 18th Dynasty, New Kingdom; Deir el-Bahri, Luxor; Upper Floor, Room 56*

Tuthmosis II was the son of Tuthmosis I and a secondary wife. He married his second sister, Hatshepsut, and reigned as king for about eighteen years. When we performed a CT-scan of this mummy we found that the king had a heart problem, and so it is possible that he died of a heart attack. The mummy had been severely damaged in antiquity by tomb robbers; both of Tuthmosis' arms were broken, as was his left leg.

## 103. The Mummy of Hatshepsut

*JE 34559; L. 155cm; 18th Dynasty, New Kingdom; Valley of the Kings, Luxor; Upper Floor, Room 56*

This mummy was found by Howard Carter in KV 60, in the Valley of the Kings. While assembling all unidentified mummies with their right arms placed across their chests – a royal posture – for the Egyptian Mummy Project, we decided to study some of them with a CT-scan machine. At the same time we also scanned a canopic box from the Deir el-Bahri cachette that was inscribed for Hatshepsut and contained her liver. To our surprise there was also a tooth inside – a molar with a root; and when we examined the mummies we found that it fit exactly into the mouth of one of the royal women. This was a beautiful moment in my life, for although it had happened by accident, I had discovered the mummy of Hatshepsut. After analysing Hatshepsut's mummy we concluded that she had died at about the age of fifty, that she had been obese, and that she had diabetes and cancer. The box that contained the tooth is also on display near the mummy.

page 182 | *103. The Mummy of Hatshepsut Mask* | *JE 34559; L. 155cm; 18th Dynasty, New Kingdom; Valley of the Kings, Luxor; Upper Floor, Room 56*

## 104. The Mummy of Tuthmosis IV

*JE 34559; L. 164cm; 18th Dynasty, New Kingdom; Valley of the Kings, Luxor; Upper Floor, Room 56*

Tuthmosis IV became king after the death of his father, Amenhotep II. He was not the intended heir to the throne as his mother was a secondary queen.  On his Dream Stele, erected between the paws of the sphinx, Tuthmosis explains how, as a young man, he would go hunting for wild animals in the valley of the gazelles around the sphinx. One day he fell asleep beside this monument, and it appeared to him in a dream as the god Ra-Horakhety. The sphinx explained to Tuthmosis that if he cleared away the sand from around his body, he would make him king of Egypt. Tuthmosis did as the god instructed and removed the sand from the sphinx, and restored the Old Kingdom stones to its body. It is possible that in this text, Tuthmosis is emphasising that the god chose him to be king, even though he was not the intended heir. Tuthmosis IV died at the age of forty-six.

## 105. The Mummy of Seti I

*JE 26213; L. 166cm; 19th Dynasty, New Kingdom; Deir el-Bahri, Luxor; Upper Floor, Room 56*

Seti I was the second king of the 19th Dynasty. He took the throne after his father, Ramesses I, and ruled for about thirteen years. No hair can be seen on the mummy's head, which has become detached from the body. It is extremely well-preserved, however.

## 106. The Mummy of Ramesses II

*JE 26214; L. 173cm; 19th Dynasty, New Kingdom; Deir el-Bahri, Luxor; Upper Floor, Room 56*

Ramesses II is the most famous king from ancient Egypt; he is particularly known for the Battle of Kadesh – a major battle between the Egyptians and the Hittites – and for the subsequent peace treaty signed by these two powerful empires. Temples, statues and tombs everywhere are covered with the name of this king. I myself found a double statue of him south of the Pyramid of Menkaure at Giza, and another at Akhmim. We have also found a temple of Ramesses II in Heliopolis in Cairo. Ramesses II died at the age of ninety-six, and his body was found in the Deir el-Bahri cache.

Under President Sadat, the mummy of Ramesses II went to Paris to be studied. It is a shame that the people there decided to keep a sample of the mummy's hair without asking for permission and that the Egyptian scholars, who accompanied the expedition, did not notice that this had happened until the son of one of the doctors tried to sell it on the internet. As soon as we discovered this, we brought the hair back to Cairo.

## 107. The Mummy of Merenptah

*JE 34562; L. 171cm; 19th Dynasty, New Kingdom; Valley of the Kings, Luxor; Upper Floor, Room 56*

Merenptah was the thirteenth son of Ramesses II. He began his reign at an old age, and died at about seventy years old. There were many wars during his reign, some of which are recorded on an important artefact known as the Israel Stele, which bears the first reference to Israel on an Egyptian monument.

This mummy was moved to the Egyptian Museum in 1907. It is in a generally good condition, although much damage was caused to the body by tomb robbers in antiquity; notably, there is a hole in the right side of the head, and the fingers of the left hand are broken, with some even missing.

JE 95316

# The Funerary Assemblage of Yuya and Tuya *(Upper Floor, Hall 43)*

*The objects on display in this room were found by James Quibell and Theodore Davis in Tomb KV 46 - in the Valley of the Kings - in 1867; together they form the virtually intact funerary assemblage of Yuya and Tuya, parents of the 18th Dynasty Queen Tiye, wife of Amenhotep III. Yuya held important military positions, such as Charioteer Commander, while Tuya was Priestess of Hathor and Amun. Although the tomb had been robbed in antiquity, evidenced by the coffins having been opened, the tomb had been resealed following the break-in, preserving the remaining contents for posterity.*

*The tomb was divided into two sections: the first, to the north, was a store, while the second section, to the south, was for the coffins and funerary objects. The sarcophagus of Yuya was located in the east, and that of Tuya in the west. Yuya's mummy was found within four coffins, all enclosing one another, and all placed within his large sarcophagus. Tuya's coffin was placed within two anthropoid coffins, themselves within her large sarcophagus. Each mummy wore an elaborate golden mask and exquisite collars, and both were provided with four alabaster canopic jars to contain the viscera. Yuya had fourteen shabti statues, compared to Tuya's four, with more than half of these fourteen statues being found inside painted boxes. Each had associated tools made from wood or copper. Yuya's Book of the Dead was also found in the tomb; this was 10m long, and describes his journey to the next life in detail. Around the sarcophagi were further funerary objects: three lion-legged chairs; a chair that had belonged to Princess Sitamun, daughter of Amenhotep III and Tiye; jewellery boxes; about twenty-seven sealed vessels; fifty-two pottery vessels filled with natron; eighteen boxes of food; and a chariot that had belonged to Sitamun.*

## 108. A Statue of Yuya in the Shape of a ba-Bird
*JE 95312; Painted limestone; H. 13.5cm; 18th Dynasty, New Kingdom; Valley of the Kings, Luxor; Upper Floor, Hall 43*

This statue represents the ba-soul of Yuya. This aspect of the soul was depicted as a bird with a human head; in this form the deceased could travel throughout the earth and the afterlife. Yuya's face is painted red, but his wings are green, and his body yellow. He wears a necklace with a heart-shaped pendant hanging from it.

## 109. The Funerary Mask of Tuya
*JE 95254; gilded cartonnage inlaid with glass and semiprecious stones; H. 40cm; 18th Dynasty, New Kingdom; Valley of the Kings, Luxor; Upper Floor, Hall 43*

When discovered this mask was covered in a thin layer of linen gauze. This was removed during restoration in 1982, but remains of the linen can still be seen in the blackened areas. Tuya is shown here wearing a long wig, while below she wears a wide collar of six rows of coloured glass and gold. Her eyes are of quartz and blue glass.

page 188 | *108. A Statue of Yuya in the Shape of a ba-Bird* | *JE 95312; Painted limestone; H. 13.5cm; 18th Dynasty, New Kingdom; Valley of the Kings, Luxor; Upper Floor, Hall 43*
page 187 | *109. The Funerary Mask of Tuya* | *JE 95254; gilded cartonnage inlaid with glass and semiprecious stones; H. 40cm; 18th Dynasty, New Kingdom; Valley of the Kings, Luxor; Upper Floor, Hall 43*

186

JE 95290

JE 95312

J.95366.

189

## 110. The Funerary Mask of Yuya

*JE 95316; gilded cartonnage; H. 33cm; 18th Dynasty, New Kingdom; Valley of the Kings, Luxor; Upper Floor, Hall 43*

This gilded cartonnage mask shows Yuya wearing a long wig. His eyebrows and eyes are inlaid with blue glass, marble and obsidian, and he wears an elaborate collar that goes beneath his wig; it consists of eleven rows of golden beads, and ends in tear-drop shaped pendants. The inside of the mask is covered in bitumen.

## 111. The Shabtis and Shabti Boxes

*JE 95366; wood; H. 30.5cm; JE 68990; wood; H. 26.2cm; JE 68983; wood; H. 27.8cm; 18th Dynasty, New Kingdom; Valley of the Kings, Luxor; Upper Floor, Hall 43*

Thirteen shabti boxes, some containing shabti figurines, were found in the tomb of Yuya and Tuya, with four boxes inscribed specifically for Yuya. They have square bases, with sides that rise higher than their vaulted lids, and door knobs to open the boxes. A further knob, above the door, would be used to seal the door. They are painted with horizontal bands of blue, green, and red on the exterior, forming panels, but are yellow inside.

Eighteen shabtis were found in the tomb, fourteen for Yuya and four for Tuya. They are all finely modelled, and have painted eyes. They are each carved from different types of wood: ebony, pine, cedar, and a commoner form of a wood painted to imitate cedar. Each is inscribed with Chapter Six of the book of the Dead, known as the Shabti Text, in which the spell causes the statuette to perform work for the deceased in the afterlife. The shabtis were also accompanied by miniature tools.

## 112. The Imitation Jars

*JE 95259; H. 24cm; JE 95282; H. 14.3cm; JE 95277; H. 21cm; painted wood; 18th Dynasty, New Kingdom; Valley of the Kings, Luxor; Upper Floor, Hall 43*

The tomb of Yuya and Tuya contained twenty-seven wooden imitation jars. Some are painted in imitation of stone vessels, others imitate glass. They take various shapes, from cylindrical to long necked.

## 113. A Tall Egyptian Alabaster Vase of Yuya and Tuya

*JE 95290; Egyptian alabaster; H. 20cm; 18th Dynasty, New Kingdom; Valley of the Kings, Luxor; Upper Floor, Hall 43*

This large vase originally contained an oily substance, and was sealed by a piece of linen, tied with string. It is distinctive because of its long neck and wide projecting rim. The handle takes the form of two papyrus stalks tied together.

## 114. The Chariot of Yuya

*CG 51188; wood, gold, leather; L. 245cm; 18th Dynasty, New Kingdom; Valley of the Kings, Luxor; Upper Floor, Hall 43*

This extremely well-preserved chariot probably belonged to Yuya, although it is not inscribed. The frame of the chariot cabin is semi-circular; the floor lined with leather. The front, sides and back are decorated with red leather, while gilt leather can also be seen, decorated with rosette patterns. The wheels are each formed of two pieces of bent wood tied together, with tyres of leather. The pole in front of the cabin is about 2m long.

## 115. The Innermost Coffin of Yuya

*JE 95228, JE 68962; wood, silver, gold, glass, semiprecious stones; L. 204cm; 18th Dynasty, New Kingdom; Upper Floor, Hall 43*

Yuya is presented wearing a wig, with the lines of his eyes and eyebrows inlaid with blue glass paste; the eyes themselves are formed from alabaster, with pupils of black glass paste. The face and ears are finely modelled, and he wears a wide collar around his neck. Below can be seen the goddess Nekhbet, spreading her wings out in protection and holding the shen-symbol of infinity in her claws. Further below is the Goddess Nut with her arms raised, her body stretching for most of the length of the coffin; on either side of her are vertical rows of hieroglyphs. The four sons of Horus can be seen on the sides of the coffin, accompanied by Thoth, while Isis can be seen at the feet, kneeling on the hieroglyphic symbol for gold. This coffin is unusual because it lacks the hands of the deceased. The inside is lined with silver.

## 116. The Black Outer Coffin of Yuya

*JE 95226; wood, gold, bitumen; L. 275cm; 18th Dynasty, New Kingdom; Valley of the Kings, Luxor; Upper Floor, Hall 43*

This black and gold anthropoid coffin shows Yuya in the form of a mummy, wearing a long wig with his arms crossed across his chest. The eyes and eyebrows are inlaid with dark blue glass, obsidian and marble. He also wears a wide golden collar; below can be seen a vulture – the goddess Nekhbet - holding the shen-sign of infinity in each claw. Bands of golden hieroglyphs spread across the coffin: one central band, and four horizontal. On the right side can be seen the gods Imsety, Anubis, Duamutef, and Geb, while on the left side can be seen Hapi, Anubis, Qebehsenuef, and Nut. The goddess Isis can be seen at the foot of the coffin.

## 117. The Golden Jewellery Box of Tuya

*JE 95248; wood, ivory, gold; H. 41cm; 18th Dynasty, New Kingdom; Valley of the Kings, Luxor; Upper Floor, Hall 43*

This box, which contained Tuya's jewellery, was discovered to the left of the entrance of the tomb. It stands on four legs and has a vaulted lid, while the decoration is formed from faience and ivory. The surface is decorated with hieroglyphic inscriptions and two scenes; the lower scene on the lid depicts the god Heh kneeling on the symbol for gold, while the upper scene displays the cartouches of Amenhotep III. Along the sides of the box are the names and titles of Amenhotep III and Queen Tiye, below which can be seen rows of golden ankh-signs standing above a basket, holding was-sceptres – together these can be read, 'all life and prosperity.'

JE 95228

CG 51188

JE 95226

JE 95248

## The Second Mummy Room *(Upper Floor, Room 52)*

### 118. The Mummy of Queen Nodjmet

*CG 61087; L. 155cm; 21st Dynasty, Third Intermediate Period; Deir el-Bahri, Luxor; Upper Floor, Room 52*

Queen Nodjmet was the wife of Herihor, the High Priest of Amun and king at Thebes in the 21st Dynasty. Her body was found in the Deir el-Bahri cachette. New mummification techniques can be seen here, notably her face has been packed full of sawdust, in order to keep its shape, and her eyebrows are artificial. Her nose is stuffed with resin, and she wears a wig.

### 119. The Mummy of Queen Henutawy

*CG 61090; L. 152cm; 21st Dynasty, Third Intermediate Period; Deir el-Bahri, Luxor; Upper Floor, Room 52*

Henutawy was the wife of Pinudjem I of the 21st Dynasty. Her mummy was found in the Deir el-Bahri cache. A golden embalming plate was found inside the stomach of the queen, bearing the eye of Horus, the names of the four sons of Horus, and an inscription including the name of the queen. Her body exhibits many of the new techniques that developed for mummification in the Third Intermediate Period, notably the subcutaneous packing of linen and sawdust to preserve the shape of the body. In this case, however, the face of the mummy had burst due to being too tightly packed; it was restored to its original form in 1974.

### 120. The Mummy of Ramesses V

*JE 34566; L. 177cm; 20th Dynasty, New Kingdom; Valley of the Kings, Luxor; Upper Floor, Room 52*

Ramesses V was the son of Ramesses III. He took the throne after his brother, Ramesses IV, but only reigned for four years, dying at the age of twenty. He appears to have suffered from a skin disease.

page 197 | *118. The Mummy of Queen Nodjmet | CG 61087; L. 155cm; 21st Dynasty, Third Intermediate Period; Deir el-Bahri, Luxor; Upper Floor, Room 52*
page 199 | *119. The Mummy of Queen Henutawy | CG 61090; L. 152cm; 21st Dynasty, Third Intermediate Period; Deir el-Bahri, Luxor; Upper Floor, Room 52*
page 198 | *120. The Mummy of Ramesses V | JE 34566; L. 177cm; 20th Dynasty, New Kingdom; Valley of the Kings, Luxor; Upper Floor, Room 52*

198

## 121. A Troop of Nubian Soldiers

*CG 257; painted wood; H. 55cm; 11th Dynasty, Middle Kingdom; Asyut; Upper Floor, Room 37*

This wooden model of marching Nubian troops was discovered in 1894 inside the tomb of Meshety, Mayor of the 13th Nome of Upper Egypt, at Asyut in Middle Egypt. Forty wooden Nubian figures are shown, walking in four rows, with short kilts, decorated in red, yellow and green. Each figure is individually carved, giving each a unique appearance, and carries a bow in one hand and arrows in the other. They are barefooted.

## 122. A Troop of Egyptian Soldiers

*CG 258; painted wood; H.59cm; 11th Dynasty, Middle Kingdom; Asyut; Upper Floor, Room 37*

As with the Nubian soldiers, described above, this model of a group of Egyptian soldiers was found in the tomb of Meshety of the 11th Dynasty. Forty soldiers can be seen, in four rows, each walking barefoot, wearing a short kilt, and carrying a pike and a cow-hide shield. They have short hair styles.

## 123. An Offering Bearer

*JE 46725; painted wood; H. 123cm; 11th Dynasty, Middle Kingdom; Deir el-Bahri, Luxor; Upper Floor, Room 27*

This wooden statue was discovered during the Metropolitan Museum's excavations in 1919 – 1920 in the Theban tomb of Meketre (TT 280). She holds a duck in her right hand, while her left hand is helping to steady a basket on her head, which contains four sealed jars of wine. Her dress is red and green, with shoulder straps, under which can be seen an elaborate collar. She also wears bracelets and anklets.

## 124. A Model Depicting a Cattle Census

*JE 46724; painted wood; H. 55.5cm; 11th-12th Dynasty, Middle Kingdom; Deir el-Bahri, Luxor; Upper Floor, Room 27*

This model was found in the tomb of Meketre at Thebes, and represents a cattle census. The cows can be seen being herded past the columned kiosk of Meketre by men with sticks, who also control the cattle by ropes tied around their horns. Within the kiosk four scribes can be seen squatting on the floor with their scribal equipment, as well as Meketre himself sitting on a chair, and Meketre's son.

## 125. A Model of a Fishing Scene

*JE 46715; painted wood; H. 31.5cm; 11th Dynasty, Middle Kingdom; Deir el-Bahari, Luxor; Upper Floor, Room 27*

Two groups of fishermen can be seen here in boats made from papyrus. Between the two boats they hold a large net for catching fish. Two men on each boat are rowing, six men are holding the net, while a further man is laying out the fish they have caught on the deck of one of the boats. Fish can also be seen in the net. This model was found in the 11th Dynasty tomb of Meketre in Thebes.

201

# The Funerary Assemblages of Maiherperi and Sennedjem

*This room contains the almost intact funerary equipment from two New Kingdom tombs – the 18th Dynasty tomb of Maiherperi in the Valley of the Kings, and the 19th Dynasty tomb of Sennedjem at Deir el-Medina in Luxor. The tomb of Maiherperi (KV 36) was found intact by Victor Loret in 1899 in the Valley of the Kings. Although the tomb is uninscribed, the stylistic evidence of the burial assemblage suggests that Maiherperi lived under Amenhotep III. In life he had been a Fanbearer on the Right of the King, an important honorific position, and a Child of the Royal Nursery, which meant that he grew up with princes, and the sons of important officials at court. He was probably of Nubian descent.*

*The tomb of Sennedjem (TT 1) was found at Deir el-Medina by a villager from Qurna at Luxor. Sennedjem was a Servant in the Place of Truth – a person who decorated and excavated the royal tombs in the Valley of the Kings – who lived in the 19th Dynasty during the reigns of Seti I and Ramesses II. Although the offering chapel above the burial had completely vanished, a shaft led to a sealed doorway, blocking the entrance to the burial. After entering the burial chamber, archaeologists discovered that the contents of the tomb were virtually intact. In total twenty mummies were found within, nine in well preserved coffins; all were members of Sennedjem's family.*

## 126. The Game Board of Maiherperi
*JE 33822; acacia, ebony, gold; H. 5cm; 18th Dynasty, New Kingdom; Valley of the Kings, Luxor; Upper Floor, Room 17*

This game board was found by Victor Loret in 1899. It was used for playing the game Senet; a popular game in ancient Egypt, often depicted in tombs. The board is divided into three rows of ten squares, forming a grid. There are thirteen game pieces associated with it, made from faience and limestone.

## 127. The Four Canopic Jars of Maiherperi
*JE 33780a; H. 26.7cm; JE 33780b; H. 39cm; JE 33780c; H. 40cm; JE 33780d; H. 41cm; Egyptian alabaster; 18th Dynasty, New Kingdom; Valley of the Kings, Luxor; Upper Floor, Room 17*

Each canopic jar bears an inscription at the front, dedicated to one of the sons of Horus, and has a human-headed lid. The eyes and eyebrows are painted, bringing the faces to life. Two of the jars are wrapped in cloth, but their inscriptions can still be seen.

## 128. The Book of the Dead of Maiherperi
*CG 24095; papyrus; L. 117.5; 18th Dynasty, New Kingdom; Valley of the Kings, Luxor; Upper Floor, Room 17*

This papyrus presents a series of vignettes from the Book of the Dead, known to the ancient Egyptians as the Book of Going Forth by Day. The vignette shown here in the centre contains Chapter 148, 'the spell for provisioning the blessed in the necropolis.' Seven cows and a bull, as well as four oars, are present to aid Maiherperi. At the far right of the papyrus Maiherperi can be seen adoring Osiris before a large pile of offerings.

JE 33822

CG 24095

JE 27302

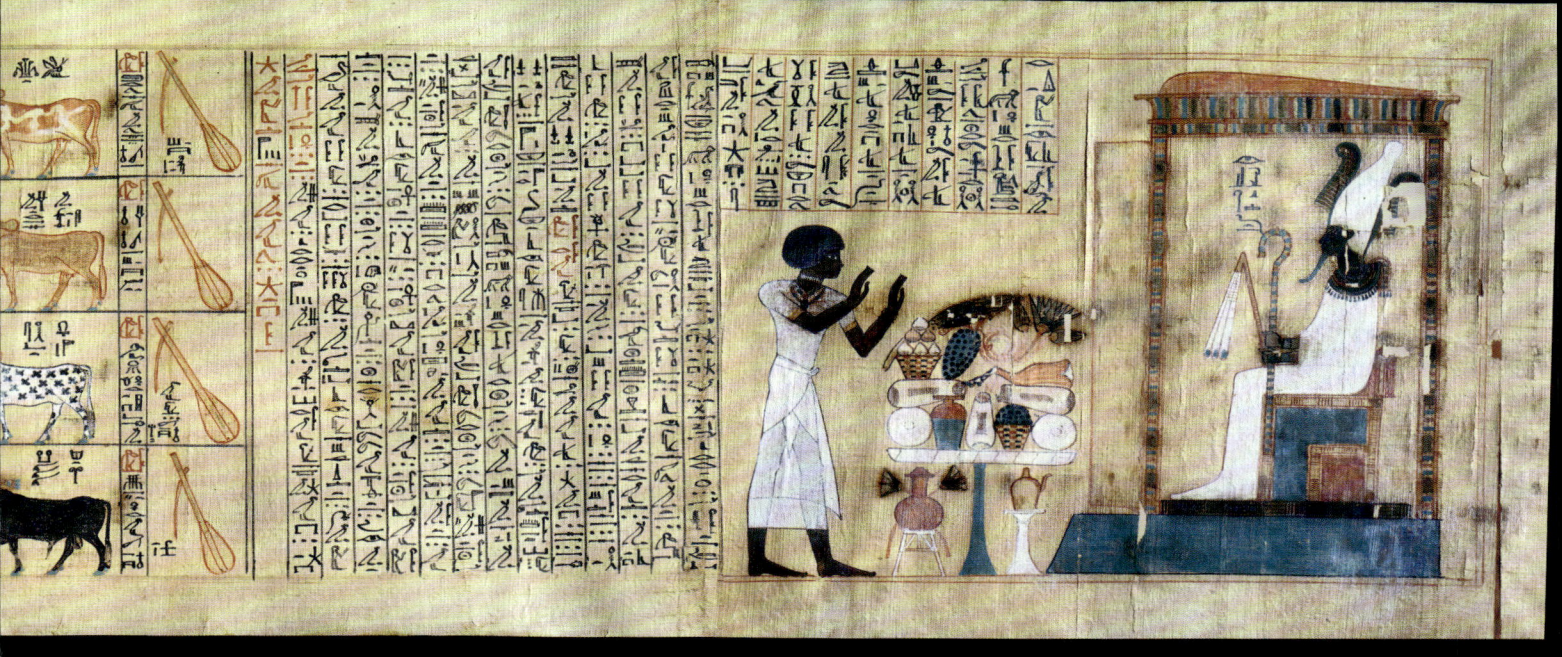

JE 33780

## 129. The Outer Sarcophagus of Khonsu

*JE 27302; wood, painted stucco; L. 248cm; 19th Dynasty, New Kingdom; Deir el-Medina, Luxor; Upper Floor, Room 17*

This wooden coffin bears decoration related to Chapter 17 of the Book of the Dead on its long sides. On one side Anubis can be seen mummifying the body of Osiris (with whom the deceased is now identified ), while Isis and Nephthys kneel at either side. Khonsu and his wife observe in the form of human-headed birds. Two lions can be seen above, with the sun-disc rising over the horizon between them. On the opposite side of the coffin, a black-skinned god represents the fertility of the Nile Valley, while Khonsu and his wife sit within a booth in the register below. At either end of the coffin the goddesses Isis, Nephthys, Selket and Neith can be seen. This coffin was found in the tomb of Sennedjem, Khonsu's father, at Deir el-Medina.

## 130. The Sarcophagus of Isis

*JE 27309; wood, cloth, painted stucco; H. 193.5cm; 19th Dynasty, New Kingdom; Deir el-Medina, Luxor; Upper Floor, Room 17*

Isis was the wife of Khabekhent, a son of Sennedjem, from Deir el-Medina. This coffin presents Isis as if she were still alive, rather than in the typical mummiform manner. She wears a heavy wig, with a large wesekh-collar below, and is wrapped in a long white tunic, from which her arms emerge. Her hands and arms are decorated with elaborate jewellery, and ivy can be seen along one side of the tunic. Her feet emerge from the tunic at the bottom of the coffin, separated by a short column of hieroglyphics.

## 131. The Door of Sennedjem's Tomb

*JE 27303; wood, painted stucco; H. 135cm; 19th Dynasty, New Kingdom; Deir el-Medina, Luxor; Upper Floor, Room 17*

This door was found blocking the entrance to the burial chamber of Sennedjem's tomb; it was still sealed with the seal of the necropolis. On the outside of the door Sennedjem and his wife can be seen in the upper register, with their daughter,  adoring the enthroned Osiris and the goddess Maat. In the lower register Sennedjem can be seen with his three sons, before Ptah-Sokar-Osiris and Isis. The inside of the door displays eleven columns of hieroglyphs, topped by a scene of Sennedjem and his wife sitting playing the game senet, in front of a pile of offerings. A part of the text is taken from Chapter 17 of the Book of the Dead, in which the deceased wishes to play Senet in the afterlife.

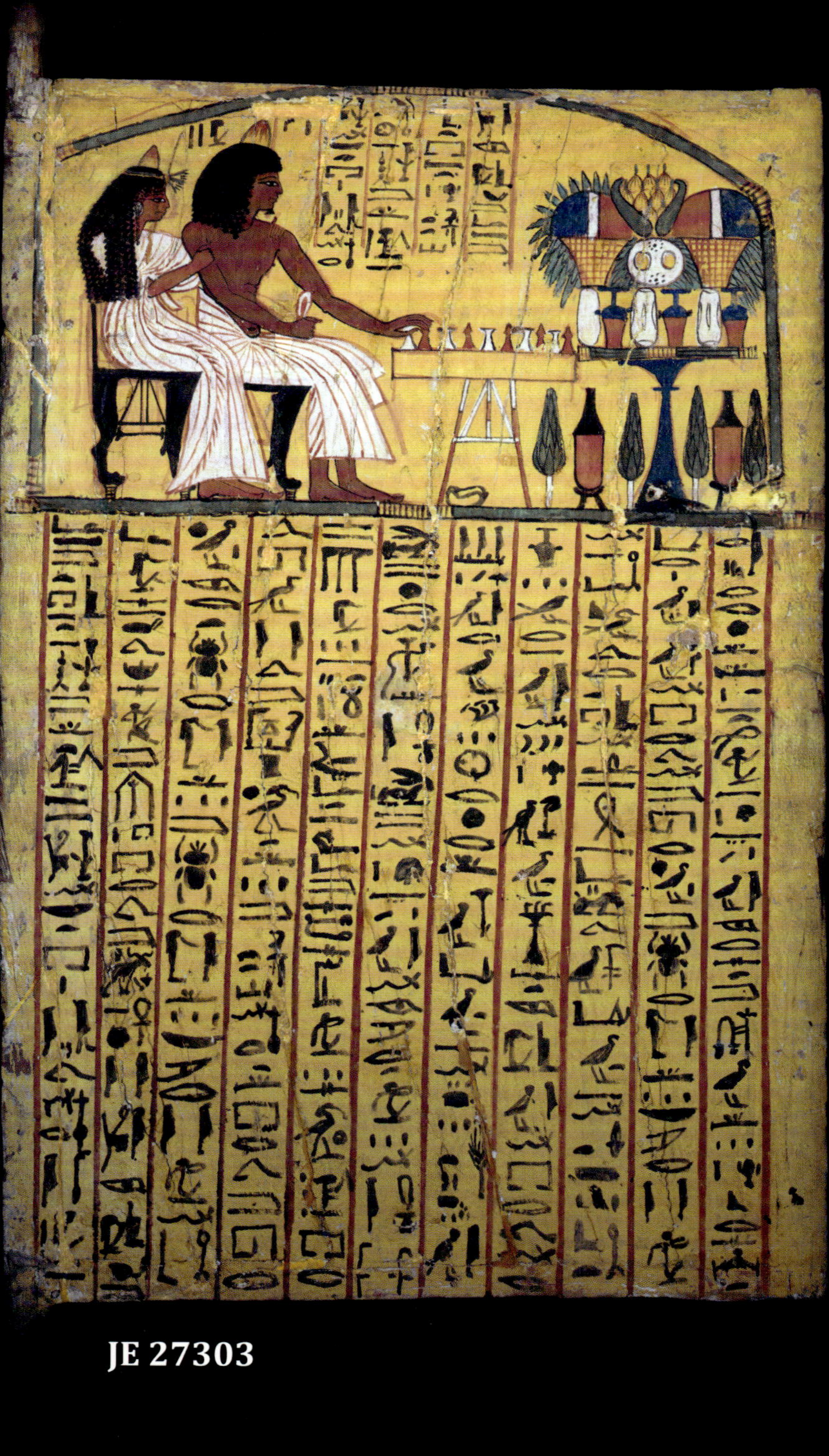

JE 27303

JE 27309

JE 85821

JE 85755 - JE 85756

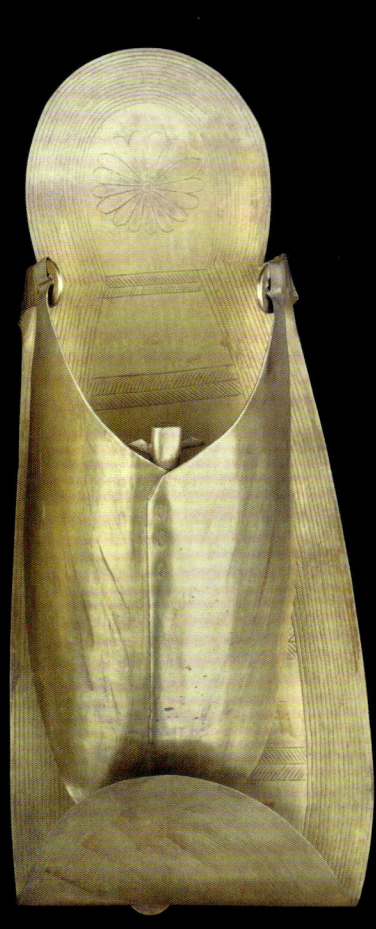

JE 85841 - JE  85842

# The Treasures of Tanis *(Upper Floor, Room 2)*

### A Brief History of the Royal Tombs of Tanis

*Tanis is an archaeological site now known as San el-Hagar, located in the Delta, northeast of Cairo. It was the capital city of the 21st and 22nd Dynasty kings of Egypt. The site attracted the attention of a number of expeditions and scholars in the Nineteenth Century, before reaching fame in 1939 when Pierre Montet discovered the royal tombs at the southwest corner of the Temple of Amun. Here was the final resting place of Kings Osorkon II, Psusennes I, Amenemopet, Shoshenk III and two unidentified kings. Within, Montet found the funerary assemblages of these kings, including their silver coffins and jewellery. These are now some of the treasures of the Egyptian Museum, and should not be missed.*

## 132. The Plaque of Psusennes I

*JE 85821; gold; H. 9.9cm; 21st Dynasty, Third Intermediate Period; Tanis; Upper Floor, Room 2*

This small golden plaque was placed over the area of the incision from which the internal organs of the deceased were removed - the purpose being to protect the body from evil. The Wadjet eye – the left eye of Horus – can be seen here, surrounded by the four sons of Horus, two to the left and two to the right; all have their arms raised in adoration. Above each god can be seen his name, while in the middle, above the Wadjet eye, can be seen the cartouche of Psusennes I.

## 133. A Necklace of King Psusennes I

*JE 85755, JE 85756; gold, lapis lazuli; L. 56cm; 21st Dynasty, Third Intermediate Period; Tanis; Upper Floor, Room 2*

This necklace is very simple; it consists of two rows of beads, made from lapis lazuli. In the middle, two golden beads can be seen, and the name of the king is found on the clasp. Curiously, one bead also has an Assyrian inscription mentioning the gods of Assur.

## 134. The Finger Stalls of Psusennes I

*JE 85822; H. 5.5cm; JE 85823; H. 6.5cm; JE 85824; H. 8cm; JE 85825; H. 6.7cm; JE 85826; H. 5.6cm; gold; 21st Dynasty, Third Intermediate Period; Tanis; Upper Floor, Room 2*

These golden finger stalls were placed over each of the mummy's fingers in order to allow him to continue to use them in the afterlife.

## 135. The Sandals of Psusennes I

*JE 85841; JE 85842; gold, L. 23.3cm; 21st Dynasty, Third Intermediate Period; Tanis; Upper Floor, Room 2*

Each sandal is divided into two parts; the upper part of each consists of two triangular sections, joined together, while the lower part is made from one shaped piece of gold. A small flower is incised at the heels. These sandals would not have been used in life, but rather are made in imitation of leather sandals.

JE 85786

JE 85822 - JE 85823 - JE 85824 - JE 85825 - JE 85826

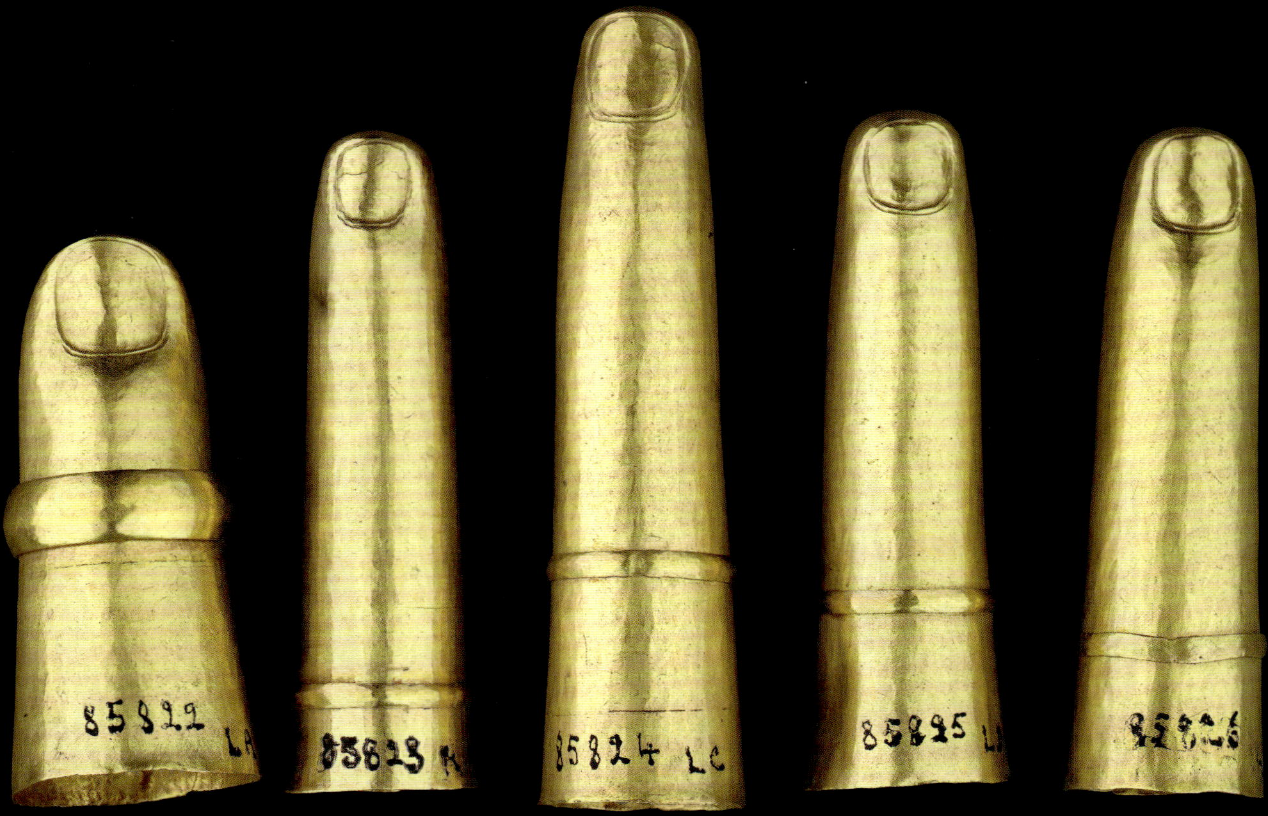

## 136. A Pectoral and Necklace of Psusennes I

*JE 85788, JE 85799; gold, red and green jasper, coloured glass, green feldspar; L. 42cm; 21st Dynasty, Third Intermediate Period; Tanis; Upper Floor, Room 2*

The pectoral here takes the form of a winged scarab, sitting above a shen-symbol, with the cartouche of the king at the front. The wings are decorated with horizontal rows of precious stones. Chapter 30 of the Book of the Dead is inscribed on the underside of the scarab, in which the deceased asks his heart not to testify against him during the judgement before Osiris. The pectoral is attached to a series of beads ending in a lotus-form counterpoise.

## 137. A Second Pectoral and Necklace of Psusennes I

*JE 85786; gold, semiprecious stones; H. 12cm; 21st Dynasty, Third Intermediate Period; Tanis; Upper Floor, Room 2*

The frame of this pectoral alternates different coloured semiprecious stones, and is topped by a cavetto cornice. Two boats can be seen at the bottom, separated by two rearing uraei. The king is shown in both boats: in one with Osiris, and in the other with the sacred benu-bird. In the central area a scarab can be seen resting on a djed-pillar. On either side are the cartouches of Psusennes I, with a shen-symbol of infinity on either side. The scarab and cartouches are protected by the goddesses Isis and Nephthys, who stand on either side stretching their arms and wings out. The pectoral is attached to a row of beads, ending in a lotus-form counterpoise.

## 138. A Third Pectoral and Necklace of Psusennes I

*JE 85791, JE 85795, JE 85796; gold, lapis lazuli, carnelian, feldspar, red jasper; H. 13.8cm; 21st Dynasty, Third Intermediate Period; Tanis; Upper Floor, Room 2*

This pectoral is framed by alternating precious stones, topped by a cavetto cornice, and with a row of alternating djed-pillar and tit-knot symbols at the bottom, below a row of sun-discs. A winged scarab can be seen in the middle, and a cartouche of the king above and below, with the uppermost cartouche surmounted by a winged sun-disc. Rearing uraei also emerge from the sun. On either side of the scarab's wings can be seen Isis and Nephthys, crouching.

## 139. A Heavy Gold Necklace of Psusennes I

*JE 85751; gold, lapis lazuli; H. 6.2cm; 21st Dynasty, Third Intermediate Period; Tanis; Upper Floor, Room 2*

Seven rings of golden threads join at a plaque, upon which can be seen a winged sun-disc and the cartouches of the king. The goddess Mut sits to one side, while Amun sits to the other. Golden chains fall from the plaque, taking the form of lotus flowers. This necklace was originally found on the mummy of Psusennes I.

JE 85791 - JE 85795 - JE 85796

219

JE 85751

## 140. A Vessel of the General Undjebauendjed

*JE 87743; silver; D. 16.5cm; 21st Dynasty, Third Intermediate Period; Tanis; Upper Floor, Room 2*

A central golden point leads to three rings of differing decoration: a rosette is followed in the next ring by lotus flowers, and then jagged lines that reach toward the rim.

## 141. A Second Vessel of the General Undjebauendjed

*JE 85904; silver and gold; D. 16cm; 21st Dynasty, Third Intermediate Period; Tanis; Upper Floor, Room 2*

The central decoration of this silver vessel takes the form of alternating flowers, emerging from a gold central point. The outer ring is formed of jagged lines that emanate towards the rim.

## 142. A Third Vessel of the General Undjebauendjed

*JE 87742; gold, silver, glass paste; D. 18.4cm; 21st Dynasty, Third Intermediate Period; Tanis; Upper Floor, Room 2*

This vessel is formed from silver, with a central section covered in gold leaf. The very centre is composed of twelve golden petals with gold paste inlay. In the next ring, four young girls can be seen, each wearing a collar, swimming in a lake full of fish, ducks and lotus flowers. An inscription on the outer ring of the vessel states that it was given to General Undjebauendjed as a gift from the king.

## 143. A Fourth Vessel of the General Undjebauendjed

*JE 87741; gold; D. 15.5cm; 21st Dynasty, Third Intermediate Period; Tanis; Upper Floor, Room 2*

This golden vessel consists of two rings of decoration. The outer ring is made of twenty-three golden grooves in the form of a flower, while the central ring is a complex pattern of papyrus and lotus flowers, formed from glass paste.

## 144. A Pendant Representing the Goddess Isis

*JE 87716; gold; H. 11cm; 21st Dynasty, Third Intermediate Period; Tanis; Upper Floor, Room 2*

This pendant represents the goddess Isis in her human form. Above her head can be seen cow's horns and a sun-disc – symbols typically associated with the goddess Hathor; however, Isis' name is found inscribed on the base. The goddess wears an elaborate collar and a long tight dress. The pendant belonged to General Undjebauendjed.

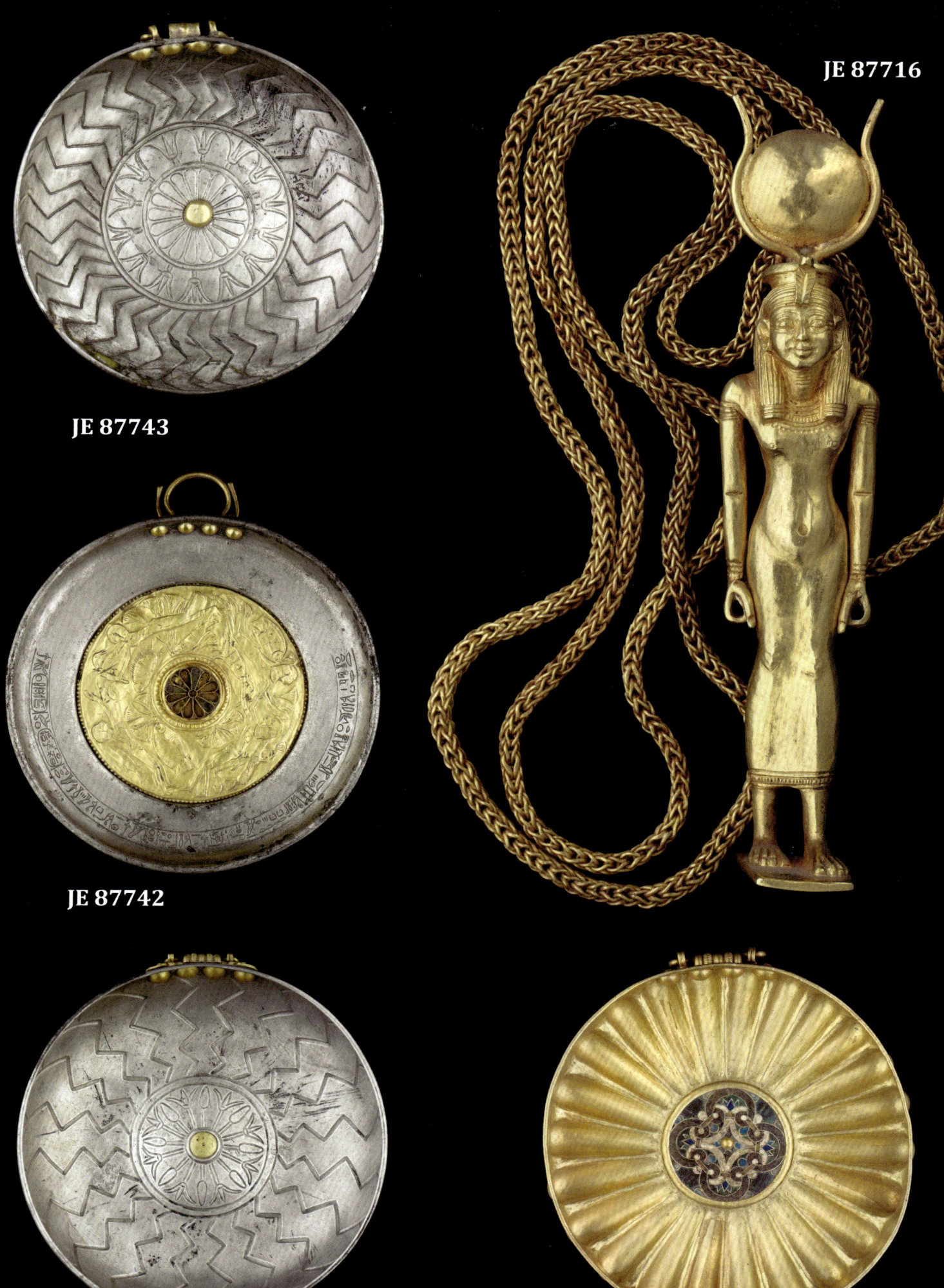

JE 87743

JE 87742

JE 85904

JE 87716

JE 87741

## 145. The Funerary Mask of Undjebauendjed

*JE 87753; gold and glass paste; H. 22cm; 21st Dynasty, Third Intermediate Period; Tanis; Upper Floor, Room 2*

This mask originally covered the face of the mummy of Undjebauendjed. Coloured glass paste forms the eyes and eyebrows. The general's face is idealised and detailed, with a slight smile.

## 146. A Pectoral of Amenemopet

*JE 86037; gold, lapis lazuli; H. 9.8cm; 21st Dynasty, Third Intermediate Period; Tanis; Upper Floor, Room 2*

The central feature of this pectoral is a lapis lazuli scarab pushing the sun-disc with its front legs. His rear legs hold the cartouche of Amenemopet. To either side, the goddesses Isis and Nephthys protect him. At the bottom of the pectoral an inscription provides the name of the king. The frame of the piece presents a winged sun-disc at the top.

## 147. Two Bracelets of Psusennes I

*JE 86027; JE 86028; gold, lapis lazuli, carnelian, green feldspar; H. 7cm; 21st Dynasty, Third Intermediate Period; Tanis; Upper Floor, Room 2*

These two bracelets are each decorated with a winged scarab as their major feature. The scarab holds the sun-disc in its front legs, and the shen-sign of infinity with its rear legs. The cartouches of Psusennes I can also be seen, each surmounted by a sun-disc. The cartouches and scarabs are separated by ovals decorated with different coloured semiprecious stones, meant to represent the wings of the scarabs.

## 148. The Funerary Mask of King Amenemopet

*JE 86059; gold, bronze, semiprecious stones; H. 30cm; 21st Dynasty, Third Intermediate Period; Tanis; Upper Floor, Room 2*

The king is shown wearing the nemes-headdress, with a uraeus formed from multiple semiprecious stones at the forehead. Bronze forms the eyebrows, the outline of the eyes, the pupils, and the edge of the face. The mask was originally part of a wooden coffin.

## 149. The Sarcophagus of Shoshenk II

*JE 72154; silver; L. 190cm; 22nd Dynasty, Third Intermediate Period; Tanis; Upper Floor, Room 2*

This silver sarcophagus takes the conventional shape of the mummified Osiris, but with the innovation of having a hawk's head in place of the human head. It belongs to King Shoshenk II, third king of the 22nd Dynasty, and was found in the tomb of Psusennes I. The hands, emerging from the mummy wrappings on the sarcophagus, hold the crook and flail – symbols of royalty, power and authority. Winged gods can be seen on the body, as well as the four sons of Horus. Four miniature silver sarcophagi were found with the sarcophagus, each was for one of the king's internal organs; these, however, have human headed.

JE 87753

JE 86037

JE 86027 - JE 86028

226

## 150. The Canopic Jars of Psusennes I

*JE 85915; H. 41cm; JE 85914; H.43cm; JE 85917; H. 39cm; JE 85916; H.38cm; alabaster and gold; 21st Dynasty, Third Intermediate Period; Tanis; Upper Floor, Room 2*

These canopic jars were found in the burial chamber of Psusennes I by Montet in 1940. They represent the four sons of Horus, and contained the viscera of the king in order to protect the organs from evil  Each god wears a gilded bronze uraeus at his forehead.

## 151. Two Bracelets of Shoshenk II

*JE 72184a-b; gold, lapis lazuli, faience, carnelian; H. 4.6cm; 22nd Dynasty, Third Intermediate Period; Tanis; Upper Floor, Room 2*

These two bracelets are identical except that one represents the wadjet eye from the right and the other from the left. The cartouches of the king can be seen within the bracelets, while, on the outside, vertical strips run along the surface, made from gold and lapis lazuli. The eye sits on a neb-basket, and is formed from lapis lazuli, with a pupil of black stone. The wadjet-eye symbol was believed to protect the wearer from harm.

## 152. A Pectoral of Shoshenk II

*JE 72171; gold, carnelian, lapis lazuli, feldspar; H. 7.7cm; H. 21st Dynasty, Third Intermediate Period; Tanis; Upper Floor, Room 2*

At its top, this pectoral displays two falcons, each wearing the double crown of Upper and Lower Egypt. They are sitting upon the hieroglyphic symbol for sky, which is adorned with stars. Below, resting upon a boat, can be seen a lapis lazuli sun-disc, with an image of the enthroned god Amun-Ra-Horakhety before the goddess Maat at its centre. To either side is a goddess, each stretching her wings out in protection: to the left is Hathor, while to the right is Maat. Plants, symbolising Upper and Lower Egypt, stand behind each. Water can be seen below the boat, represented by inlaid wavy lines. At the bottom are alternating open and closed lotuses, although the final lotus to the left is missing.

## 153. The Funerary Mask of Psusennes I

*JE 85913; gold, lapis lazuli, glass paste; H. 48cm; 21st Dynasty, Third Intermediate Period; Tanis; Upper Floor, Room 2*

This funerary mask is the most beautiful of all those found at Tanis. The king wears the nemes-headdress, with a uraeus at the forehead, and a false beard. His eyebrows and eyes are made from black and white glass paste. He also wears the wesekh-collar. The face is idealised.

229

JE 72171

JE 72184 a-b

231

# The Tutankhamun Rooms

## A Brief History of the Tutankhamun Collection

*One of the most exciting collections in the Egyptian Museum, and one that will certainly capture your heart, is the funerary assemblage of the golden boy, King Tutankhamun. Tutankhamun became king in the late 18th Dynasty following the death of King Smenkhkare, a vague character that we know little about. Tutankhamun was married to Queen Ankhesenpaaten, daughter of King Akhenaten and Queen Nefertiti. He was raised in the palaces of Amarna during the religious revolution, but, after the capital city moved backed to Thebes, he changed his name from Tutankhaten to Tutankhamun. After his death, Aye, who was a noble of great importance, became king.*

*Howard Carter discovered Tutankhamun's tomb, virtually intact, on November 4th 1922; he then spent the next ten years of his life carefully emptying it, and researching the objects within. Altogether he found 5398 objects. Carter originally came to Egypt to work as a draftsman, but later on became Inspector of Antiquities in Upper Egypt and worked in the Valley of the Kings. During this time he spent five seasons searching for the tomb of Tutankhamun, supported by Lord Carnarvon. He lived in a rest-house at the valley; this has now been converted into a museum, celebrating the history of the discovery of the tomb and the life of Howard Carter.*

*On the morning of November 4th, 1922, a young boy of fourteen was bringing water to the workmen at the valley. When placing his large water vessel on the ground he tried to make space for it by digging with his hands to remove the sand. He could not have known that he was about to enter history. While digging he found a step; straight away he ran to Carter's tent and took him by the hand to bring him to see his discovery. Carter then began to excavate with his workmen until they found the entrance to the tomb. He was so happy that his dream had come true that he immediately sent a telegram to Lord Carnarvon saying that a great discovery had been made in the valley, a completely sealed tomb, and that he would wait for his arrival.*

*Lord Carnarvon came with his daughter, Lady Evelyn, on November 23rd. On November 24th Carter took Lord Carnarvon to the tomb's entrance to show him the intact seals of the cemetery. Then, as they opened the tomb, Lord Carnarvon asked Carter what he could see inside, and Carter replied the famous words that are still known by everyone today - 'wonderful things.'*

*Hall 8*

## 154. The Second Shrine of Tutankhamun

*JE 60666 = Carter 237; wood and gold leaf; H. 225cm; 18th Dynasty, New Kingdom; Valley of the Kings, Luxor; Upper Floor, Hall 8*

This is one of the four shrines that originally housed the royal sarcophagus; the other three can be seen on display nearby. It has a sloping roof in the form of a per wer great house, which was associated with Upper Egyptian shrines. The majority of the scenes on the interior and exterior of this shrine derive from the Book of the Dead; however, scenes of Tutankhamun before Osiris and Ra-Horakhety adorn the doors, and Isis and Nephthys can be seen at the rear. On the interior ceiling is the goddess Nut upon the hieroglyph for gold, and five protective vultures. The shrine is built of sixteen parts, held together by wood and copper tenons.

page 233 | *154. The Second Shrine of Tutankhamun* | *JE 60666 = Carter 237; wood and gold leaf; H. 225cm; 18th Dynasty, New Kingdom; Valley of the Kings, Luxor; Upper Floor, Hall 8*

232

JE 60666

233

## 155. The Ceremonial Chariot of Tutankhamun

*JE 61990a = Carter 122; wood, gesso, gold leaf, semiprecious stones, glass; L. 250cm; 18th Dynasty, New Kingdom; Valley of the Kings, Luxor; Upper Floor, Hall 13*

This ceremonial chariot was found in the antechamber of the tomb along with three other chariots; six chariots were found in total within the tomb, all disassembled. The frame of this ceremonial chariot is made from wood. The cabin is decorated with golden spirals, with cartouches of the king at the top. Two uraei can be seen close to here, emerging from a decorative support attached to the shaft. The cabin's floor is formed from leather thongs, covered by animal skins. Three rows of decorative features can be seen on the interior of the cabin: the names and epithets of the king are at the top, followed by plants representing Upper and Lower Egypt. At the bottom are kneeling enemies, with ropes tied around their necks. The back of the chariot displays ornate images of the god Bes, with their ivory tongues sticking out of their mouths. The six-spoked wheels were originally lined with leather tyres.

## 156. A Collar Representing the Goddess Nut

*JE 61944 = Carter 261p(1); gold, semiprecious stones; H. 12.6cm; 18th Dynasty, New Kingdom; Valley of the Kings, Luxor; Upper Floor, Room 3*

This collar was found in the chapel of Anubis within the tomb; it shows the goddess Nut in human form with her wings and arms outstretched, protecting the cartouches of Tutankhamun. Below her wings can be seen eight rows of hieroglyphs, again related to protection by the gods. The piece is surmounted by a cavetto cornice. It has been argued by some scholars that this piece was not originally made for Tutankhamun, as the cartouches show signs of having been altered.

## 157. The Pectoral of Osiris, Isis and Nephthys

*JE 61946 = Carter 261o; gold, lapis lazuli coloured glass; H. 33cm; 18th Dynasty, New Kingdom; Valley of the Kings, Luxor; Upper Floor, Room 3*

This beautiful pectoral, made from gold and semiprecious stones, looks at first glance to be presenting the goddesses Wadjet and Nekhbet, the symbols of Upper and Lower Egypt, standing on either side of Osiris. However, the hieroglyphic inscriptions beside them state that they are in fact Isis (next to the vulture) and Nephthys (next to the cobra). Isis wears the White Crown of Upper Egypt, here associated with two feathers, making it reminiscent of the atef-crown, while Nephthys wears the Red Crown of Lower Egypt. Between their wings can be seen the shen-symbol of infinity. A cavetto cornice is at the top of the pectoral, with a long row of uraei below.

JE 61946

## 158. A Pectoral with a Winged Scarab

*JE 61888 = Carter 267p; gold, carnelian, lapis lazuli, turquoise; H. 7.5cm; 18th Dynasty, New Kingdom; Valley of the Kings, Luxor; Upper Floor, Room 3*

Here the god Khepri can be seen in the form of a scarab beetle, made from lapis lazuli. He is holding the sun-disc above his head, which is made from carnelian, and standing on a basket – the hieroglyphic sign *neb*. Together the elements of the pectoral spell out one of Tutankhamun's cartouche names – Nebkheperure.

## 159. A Pectoral of the Rising Sun

*JE 61885 = Carter 267L; gold, semiprecious stones, glass; H. 8.6cm; 18th Dynasty; New Kingdom; Valley of the Kings, Luxor; Upper Floor, Room 3*

Here can be seen a representation of the rising sun. In the middle we see the god Khepri pushing the sun-disc above his head. On either side of him are baboons, each with a lunar crescent and moon above his head. They are helping with the rebirth of the sun. Together they sit on the solar boat, framed by was-sceptres (symbol of prosperity) at either side, and the sky above them. Water is represented below the boat. Many religious symbols can be seen on the chain from which the pectoral hangs – such as Djed-pillars of stability, and ankh-signs of life.

## 160. The Golden Mask of Tutankhamun

*JE 60672 = Carter 256a; gold, lapis lazuli, quartz, carnelian, turquoise, obsidian, coloured glass; H. 54cm; 18th Dynasty, New Kingdom; Valley of the Kings, Luxor; Upper Floor, Room 3*

Please see 'my favourite objects in the museum' chapter for details about this piece.

## 161. The First (Innermost) Golden Coffin

*JE 60671 = Carter 255; gold, semiprecious stones, coloured glass; L. 187.5cm; 18th Dynasty, New Kingdom; Valley of the Kings, Luxor; Upper Floor, Room 3*

In the New Kingdom it was normal for kings and queens, as well as high officials, to have their mummies placed inside coffins, which would themselves be placed in large stone sarcophagi. The inner coffins were modelled in the shape of a mummy, and were often made of gilded wood. The mummy of King Tutankhamun was found inside a large rectangular quartzite sarcophagus, with a lid made of red granite; within were three further coffins, of which the one on display here is the innermost. The third (outermost) coffin is inside the sarcophagus within the tomb, and still contains the mummy of the king. The sarcophagus itself was found within four wooden shrines.

This beautiful golden anthropoid coffin has incised inscriptions and decoration. Tutankhamun is presented wearing the nemes-headdress, and a cobra and vulture at his forehead. Although the eyes are missing, the eye lines and eyebrows are present, inlaid with lapis lazuli. He wears an elaborate shebyu-collar around his neck, as well as a wesekh-pectoral of semiprecious stones, and holds the symbols of power and authority in his hands, crossed just below his chest. The dead king is in the posture of Osiris, as all kings would become Osiris in death. Isis and Nephthys can be seen on the lower half of the coffin, spreading out their wings in protection. Two lines of inscription run down the centre.

page 242 | *158. A Pectoral with a Winged Scarab* | *JE 61888 = Carter 267p; gold, carnelian, lapis lazuli, turquoise; H. 7.5cm; 18th Dynasty, New Kingdom; Valley of the Kings, Luxor; Upper Floor, Room 3*
pages 242-243 | *159. A Pectoral of the Rising Sun* | *JE 61885 = Carter 267L; gold, semiprecious stones, glass; H. 8.6cm; 18th Dynasty; New Kingdom; Valley of the Kings, Luxor; Upper Floor, Room 3*
page 241 | *161. The First (Innermost) Golden Coffin* | *JE 60671 = Carter 255; gold, semiprecious stones, coloured glass; L. 187.5cm; 18th Dynasty, New Kingdom; Valley of the Kings, Luxor; Upper Floor, Room 3*

JE 60671

JE 60670

JE 61885

JE 61888

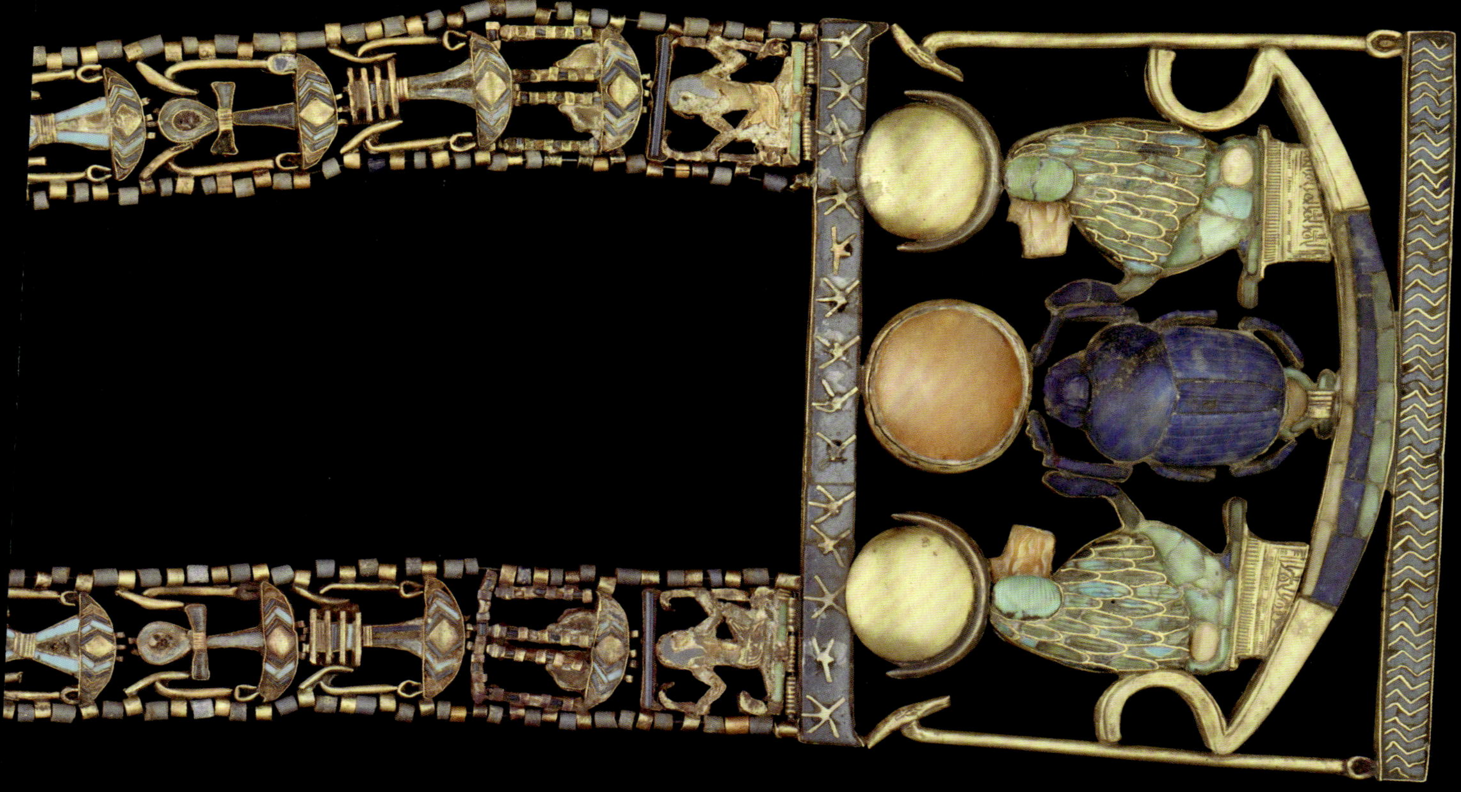

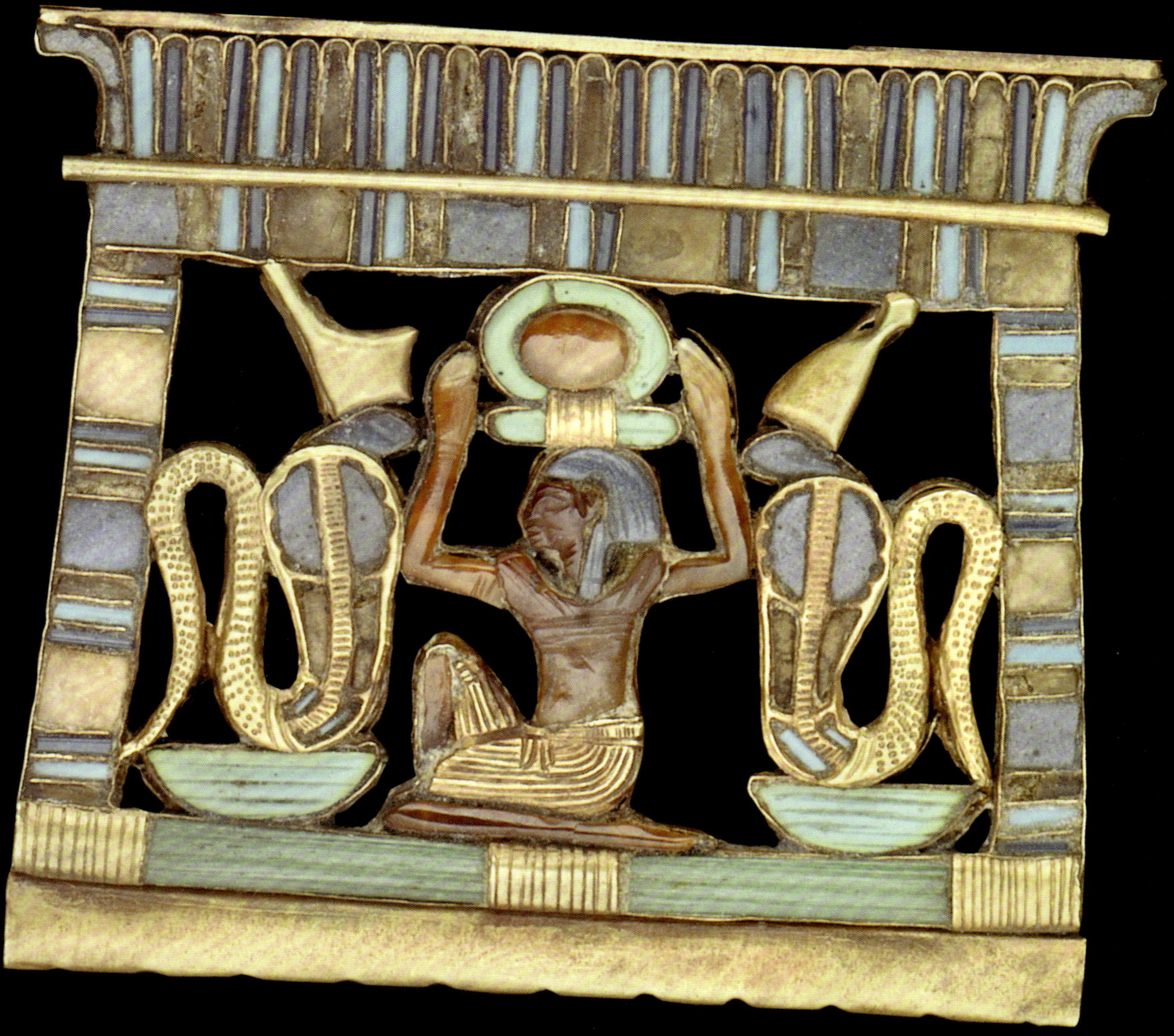

## 162. The Second Golden Coffin

*JE 60670 = Carter 254; gold, coloured glass; L. 204cm; 18th Dynasty, New Kingdom; Valley of the Kings, Luxor; Upper Floor, Room 3*

This second golden anthropoid coffin resembles the first coffin closely, except that the eyes are still present here. Again, the king is presented in the form of Osiris, wearing the nemes-headdress, with a vulture and cobra at the forehead representing Wadjet and Nekhbet. Below, he holds the crook and flail – symbols of authority and power. The majority of the coffin is covered in a feathered pattern, known as rishi. Wadjet and Nekhbet spread their wings across the body of the king in protection, holding the shen-sign of infinity in their claws.

## 163. The Corslet of Tutankhamun

*JE 62627 = Carter 054k; gold, coloured glass, ivory, carnelian; H. 40; 18th Dynasty, New Kingdom; Valley of the Kings, Luxor; Upper Floor, Room 3*

This corslet, made from numerous pieces, will have been worn on ceremonial occasions. It completely circled the torso of the king, and was worn over the shoulders and fastened there. A pendant can be seen below the collar at the front and back. At the front is the god Amun, coloured blue, standing in front of Tutankhamun offering life and the staff of years. Tutankhamun is brought to Amun by Atum, who stands in front of the Goddess Iusaas. The rear pendant displays the solar scarab, accompanied on either side by two uraei wearing the crowns of Upper Egypt and Lower Egypt respectively; each rests upon two ankh-signs. Below the pendants, the lower part of the corslet resembles feathers, made from glass beads.

*Hall 9*

## 164. The Canopic Shrine on a Sledge

*JE 60686 = Carter 266; gold and wood; H. 90cm; 18th Dynasty, New Kingdom; Valley of the Kings, Luxor; Upper Floor, Hall 9*

This canopic shrine contained the alabaster canopic chest for Tutankhamun's viscera. The goddesses Isis, Neith, Selket and Nephthys spread their arms out around the sides of the shrine, protecting it and the four sons of Horus within, who themselves protect the viscera of the king. The statues are made from gilded wood, with the eyebrows and lines around the eyes coloured black. The texts written on the sides of the shrine continue the theme of protection, while two rows of protective cobras can also be seen running along each side near the top, along with a cavetto cornice. The shrine itself sits on top of a sledge.

245

JE 60687

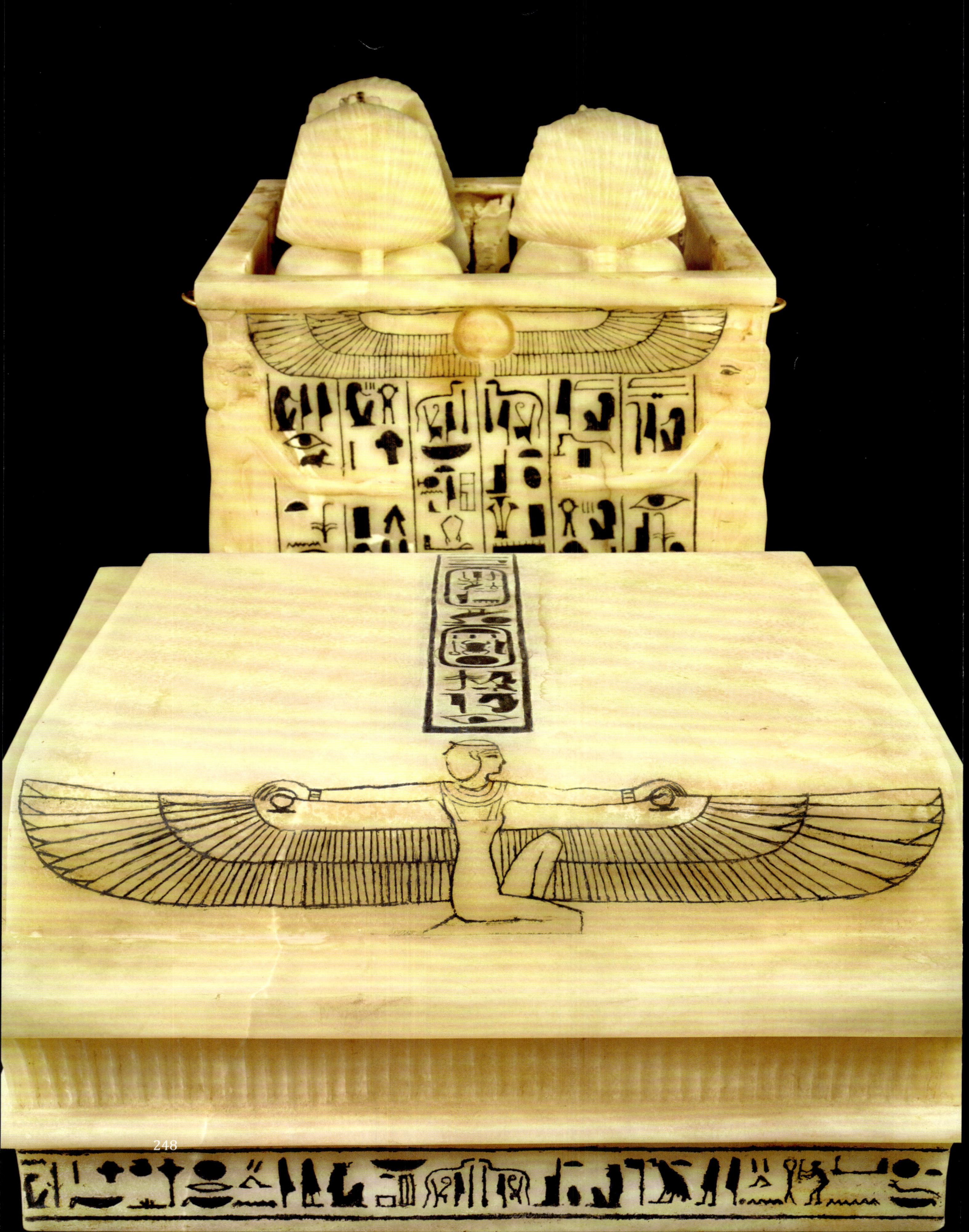

## 165. The Canopic Chest

*JE 60687 = Carter 266b; Egyptian alabaster; H. 85.5cm; 18th Dynasty, New Kingdom; Valley of the Kings, Luxor; Upper Floor, Hall 9*

This canopic chest was found within the canopic shrine, described above. As with the shrine, it is found on top of a sledge. Each corner is protected by a different goddess - Isis, Nephthys, Selket, and Neith. The chest is divided into four compartments, each with its own lid in the form of the king's head, wearing a nemes-headdress, with a uraeus and vulture at the forehead. A small golden coffinette was found within each compartment, containing the king's viscera. Djed-pillars can be seen in gold leaf at the base of the chest. It is carved from one single block of Egyptian alabaster.

## 166. Anubis above a Shrine-Shaped Box

*JE 61444 = Carter 261; painted wood, gold, silver, quartz, calcite, obsidian; H. 114cm; 18th Dynasty, New Kingdom; Valley of the Kings, Luxor; Upper Floor, Hall 9*

Here the god Anubis can be seen in his jackal form resting on a shrine-shaped box; this contains many compartments and is decorated on the exterior with alternating djed and tit-symbols. Anubis was one of the most important gods; he was seen as a guardian of the cemetery and the one who led the deceased to the next world. The shrine itself rests upon a sledge, which could be carried with four poles. The statue is carved from wood, but many parts are gilded, such as the inside of the ears and the collar.

## 167. A Headrest of King Tutankhamun

*JE 62023 = Carter 403d; Ivory; H. 19.2cm; 18th Dynasty, New Kingdom; Valley of the Kings, Luxor; Upper Floor, Hall 9*

This folding headrest bears images of the god Bes - protector of the household, women and children - on its underside, and lotus flower designs - connected to resurrection - where the pillow would be placed. The base takes the form of four ducks' heads, which are inscribed with Tutankhamun's prenomen.

## 168. A Ritual Couch in the Shape of a Lion

*JE 62011 = Carter 035; wood, gold, glass; H. 156cm; 18th Dynasty, New Kingdom; Valley of the Kings, Luxor; Upper Floor, Hall 9*

Two lions are presented here; their eyes are formed from quartz, while the areas below, as well as the noses, are made from blue glass. Their tails curl high behind the couch. There is an inscription for Mehet-Weret, the cow goddess, which is probably an indication that parts of this couch were confused with the cow-shaped couch (JE 62013) when they were being inscribed. The footboard displays djed-symbols and tit-knots.

JE 62013

253

JE 62011

JE 62012

JE 62013

JE 62012

## 169. A Ritual Couch in the Shape of Ammit

*JE 62012 = Carter 137; wood, gold, glass; H. 134cm; 18th Dynasty, New Kingdom; Valley of the Kings, Luxor; Upper Floor, Hall 10*

This ritual couch takes the form of Ammit, the devourer of souls unworthy of entering the afterlife, who is identified in an inscription at the head-end of the couch. She has the head of a hippopotamus, the tail of a crocodile and the body of a feline. This creature is well-known from Chapter 125 of the Book of the Dead, where she sits in the judgement hall of Osiris. The animal's teeth are made from ivory, as is the tongue, but this is stained red.

## 170. A Ritual Couch in the Shape of the Sky Cow

*JE 62013 = Carter 073; wood with gold, glass; H. 150cm; 18th Dynasty, New Kingdom; Valley of the Kings, Luxor; Upper Floor, Hall 10*

This ritual couch is in the shape of two cows, with spots made from opaque blue glass. Each head is surmounted by a sun-disc and horns - symbols typically associated with the goddess Hathor; however, the cow is the goddess Mehet-Weret, the Great Flood, associated with the creation of the world. The eyes are inlaid with glass paste, and take the form of wadjet-eyes – connecting the couch to the god Horus. This couch, like all three ritual couches found in the tomb, can be taken apart into four pieces consisting of the couch itself, the two animal-shaped side supports, and a footboard, which all attached to a rectangular base.

## 171. A Small Wooden Image of the King on a Bier

*JE 60720 = Carter 331a; wood; L. 42cm; 18th Dynasty, New Kingdom; Valley of the Kings, Luxor; Upper Floor, Hall 15*

This wooden effigy of the king was found within a black wooden box. It was given as a gift to the king by the Overseer of the Treasury, Maya, evidenced by the horizontal inscription on the base of the piece. The king can be seen lying on a bier, which takes the form of two lions side by side. He wear the nemes-headdress, with a uraeus at the forehead, and a broad collar. Two birds can be seen spreading their wings over him in protection; the one to his left is the ba-soul, while the one to his right is either the god Horus or an image of the ka (life-force). The king's hands emerge from the birds' outstretched wings. A central band of hieroglyphs, asking the goddess Nut for protection, run down the centre of the effigy to the feet, while three horizontal bands cross it.

## 172. A Model Boat

*JE 61331 = Carter 334; painted wood; L. 108cm; 18th Dynasty, New Kingdom; Valley of the Kings, Luxor; Upper Floor, Hall 15*

This model represents a reed boat. The stem and stern both curve upwards and are painted red, followed by feathered patterns, circles and chequers. Overall, however, the boat is painted yellow. There is a large cabin at its centre; this has an entrance at either long side, and displays a cavetto cornice along its upper edges. It is decorated with a colourful chequered pattern, the roof is white, and there are no windows. The mast at the centre of the boat is fully rigged, and originally held a square sail. At the stern one large oar can be seen, which is fixed to the ship.

JE 61331

JE 60720

257

## 173. A Boat with Two Figures

*JE 62120 = Carter 578; Egyptian alabaster; H. 37cm; 18th Dynasty, New Kingdom; Valley of the Kings, Luxor; Upper Floor, Hall 20*

This model has been made in the form of a boat, resting upon an inner stand within a tank. The head of a gazelle can be seen at each end of the boat; both have pierced ears, collars inlaid with gold, real horns, and face the same direction. At the centre is a cabin with four elaborate columns and screen walls. At the prow and stern are figures, one standing and one sitting. The standing figure is a female dwarf, while the seated figure is a servant girl, holding an ivory lotus flower; both wear curly wigs. The tank is decorated with geometric and floral patterns, as well as the names of the king and queen. A uraeus can be seen to either side of the cartouches, one wearing the crown of Upper Egypt, the other the crown of Lower Egypt.

## 174. A Perfume Vessel

*JE 62114 = Carter 210; Egyptian alabaster, ivory and gold; H. 70.5cm; 18th Dynasty, New Kingdom; Valley of the Kings, Luxor; Upper Floor, Hall 20*

This vessel was carved in the shape of the hieroglyphic symbol sema, representing the unification of Upper and Lower Egypt. Two Nile gods can be seen tying the symbols of the north and south – the papyrus and lotus - together. Two stems of papyrus behind the figures are surmounted by cobras, one wearing the Red Crown of Lower Egypt, and the other wearing the White Crown of Upper Egypt. The names of both Tutankhamun and his wife, Ankhesenamun, can be seen in the middle of the vessel, while Tutankhamun's cartouche is protected by two solar falcons at the bottom.

## 175. A Vessel in the Form of a Standing Lion

*JE 62124 = Carter 579; Egyptian alabaster; H. 60cm; 18th Dynasty, New Kingdom; Valley of the Kings, Luxor; Upper Floor, Hall 20*

This lion shaped vessel for perfume, or some form of unguent, wears an elaborate floral crown that acted as a lid. It has gilded eyes, and its nose was originally painted blue. Details of the mane are incised into the stone, while its red tongue and teeth are made from ivory. The lion raises its right paw, almost in greeting, while its left arm rests upon the hieroglyphic symbol *sah* meaning protection. On the chest are the names of Tutankhamun and Ankhesenamun. It stands on a pedestal, which resembles a jar stand.

## 176. The Ritual Chair

*JE 62030 = Carter 351; ebony, ivory, gold, faience, semi-precious stones; H. 102cm; 18th Dynasty, New Kingdom; Valley of the Kings, Luxor; Upper Floor, Hall 25*

The complicated decoration of this folding chair consists of inlays of ebony, ivory, faience and semiprecious stones. The cartouches of the king can be seen at either side of the upper part of the chair back; between them the vulture goddess spreads out her wings in protection, with shen-signs of infinity below her. Around the edges of the seat can be seen ivory inlays, made in imitation of animal skin. The legs of the chair are in the form of duck's heads.

JE 62124

## 177. The Head of King Tutankhamun Emerging from a Lotus

*JE 60723 = Carter 008; painted wood; H. 30cm; 18th Dynasty, New Kingdom; Valley of the Kings, Luxor; Upper Floor, Hall 30*

Howard carter found this piece, which represents the king as the god Nefertum, at the entrance of the corridor leading into the tomb. It is probable that this was not its original location, and so it may have been moved by thieves at some point in antiquity. The king's head can be seen emerging from a lotus, which was an important symbol of birth and resurrection in ancient Egypt; he is shown shaven-headed, with pierced ears.

## 178. A Chest with Hunting and Battle Scenes

*JE 61467 = Carter 021; wood; H. 44 cm; 18th Dynasty, New Kingdom; Valley of the Kings, Luxor; Upper Floor, Hall 35*

This famous chest, which was found to contain garments, is extremely well preserved. The lid is decorated with scenes of the king hunting on his chariot, firing arrows from his bow, while the animals all run away from him in fear. At the front and rear of the chest Tutankhamun, shown on a large scale, is shown attacking different groups of enemies; on one side he fights Nubians, while on the other it is Asiatics. All fall down in confusion and chaos before him as he, and the marching Egyptian army behind, move in perfect order. All the while the king is protected by two vultures flying above him, and cooled by fan-bearers walking behind. The associated inscriptions present him as strong and brave. The scenes are framed by geometric patterns.

## 179. The Throne of King Tutankhamun

*JE 62028 = Carter 091; wood, gold, silver, glass, and semiprecious stones; H. 100cm; 18th Dynasty, New Kingdom; Valley of the Kings, Luxor; Upper Floor, Hall 35*

This is one of the most impressive objects in the museum, and shows clearly how the ancient artists had reached a peak of skill and ability. This beautiful wooden chair is covered in a thin layer of gold, with inlays of semiprecious stones and silver. The arms are modelled in the form of winged snakes, wearing the Double Crown of Upper and Lower Egypt, guarding the two cartouches of Tutankhamun. The chair legs are made in the form of lion's paws, and are also topped with lion's heads. On the front of the throne is a beautiful scene of Queen Ankhesenpaaten leaning with affection towards her husband, who is seated on a chair; she touches him gently with one hand, and holds a perfume vessel in the other. The king is shown here wearing a wig and a complex crown; below he wears a long kilt. Between both figures the Aten shines its rays down upon them. A row of four uraei can be seen on the back of the throne.

## 180. A Statue of King Tutankhamun on the Back of a Tiger
*JE 60714 = Carter 289b; painted wood, gold; H. 85.6cm; 18th Dynasty, New Kingdom; Valley of the Kings, Luxor; Upper Floor, Hall 45*

This is one of thirty-four wooden statues found in a chest within the tomb. It shows the king wearing the White Crown of Upper Egypt, with a uraeus at the forehead, a wide wesekh-collar, a short kilt, and golden sandals. In his left hand he holds a long stick, while in his right he holds a flail – a symbol of authority. His face and body were modelled in the typical Amarna style. The king stands on a base above a black tiger – a symbol of the night sky to the ancient Egyptians, and thus of the underworld. The king, shining golden, stands above the tiger, emphasising his domination and rebirth.

## 181. Two Figures of the God Ihy
*JE 60731 = Carter 289c, JE 60732 = Carter 275a; wood, resin, calcite; H. 60.5cm; 18th Dynasty, New Kingdom; Valley of the Kings, Luxor; Upper Floor, Hall 45*

These two un-inscribed naked figures are thought to represent the god Ihy, a sky god linked with rebirth, who was also the son of the goddess Hathor. They each show the god as a naked child, covered in black resin, with gilded eyebrows. Each is shaven-headed, with a side-lock of youth descending over the right shoulder, and holds a golden sistrum in the right hand.

## 182. A Statue of Sekhmet
*JE 60749 = Carter 300a; wood, gesso, gold, glass; H. 55.2cm; 18th Dynasty, New Kingdom; Valley of the Kings, Luxor; Upper Floor, Hall 45*

This wooden statue was covered with gesso and painted. It depicts the goddess Sekhmet sitting on a backless throne. Her head is surmounted by a sun-disc and a wig that falls down onto her breasts; between the ends of the wig can be seen an elaborate collar. Her eyes and nose are inlaid with glass. She wears a tight dress, which is formed from a beaded-pattern, and is identified by an inscription on the pedestal.

## 183. A Guardian Statue of King Tutankhamun
*JE 60708 = Carter 029; wood covered with resin, bronze and gold; H. 192cm; 18th Dynasty, New Kingdom; Valley of the Kings, Luxor; Upper Floor, Hall 45*

This wooden statue, one of two originally found in the tomb, acted as a guardian to the burial chamber. The black colour of the statue's skin connects it with the god Osiris and rebirth. It wears the khat-headdress, with a uraeus at the forehead, and jewellery in the form of a broad collar, a pectoral, and bracelets. It strides forward with its left leg, and wears gilded bronze sandals. It holds a mace in its right hand, and a staff in its left. The second statue differs only in that it wears the nemes-headdress, rather than the khat.

JE 60731

JE 60732

JE 60714

# The Jewellery Room (Upper Floor, Room 4)

### Jewellery in Ancient Egypt

*Jewellery manufacture began in the Neolithic Period, and reached its peak in the Middle Kingdom; however, great pieces were still created after this time, such as the items in the tomb of Tutankhamun, and the treasures from Tanis. It served the function of protecting the wearer from hidden powers; so we see the Egyptians wearing objects around their necks, arms, feet, or any part of the body regarded as weak. As time progressed jewellery became more decorative, used to enhance the beauty of the owner, with artisans using gold, silver, and semiprecious stones to create their elaborate pieces.*

*The jewellery worn by the ancient Egyptians falls into two categories: that which served a decorative purpose - used to show a person's rank in society; and that which was used to protect the deceased in the afterlife. These latter items could also be used in daily life, and then buried in the tomb at the time of death; however, there is often a difference between the jewellery used in life and that placed in the tomb – typically the materials used and the size of the piece.*

## 184. The Bracelets from the Tomb of King Djer

*JE 35054; gold, turquoise, lapis lazuli, amethyst; Max L. 18cm; 1st Dynasty, Early Dynastic Period; Abydos; Upper Floor, Room 4*

These four bracelets were discovered by Flinders Petrie at Abydos, attached to the remains of a female arm; they may thus have all belonged to the same princess. They are beautifully made, and show the high quality of work that was already being produced as early as the 1st Dynasty.

## 185. A Girdle of Mereret

*JE 30879, JE 30923; gold, amethyst, L. 60cm; 12th Dynasty, Middle Kingdom; Dashur; Upper Floor, Room 4*

This girdle is composed of dual rows of beads, alternating with carefully modelled panther heads. These are very detailed, and served the function of protecting the wearer from harm.

## 186. A Pendant of Mereret

*JE 53070; gold, turquoise, lapis lazuli, carnelian; H. 4.6cm; 12th Dynasty, Middle Kingdom; Dashur; Upper Floor, Room 4*

The centre of this pendant is made from carnelian. Above can be seen a lotus flower, and below, curving around the carnelian centre, is a floral pattern of turquoise and lapis lazuli. The outer section is golden.

pages 274-275 | ***184. The Bracelets from the Tomb of King Djer*** | *JE 35054; gold, turquoise, lapis lazuli, amethyst; Max L. 18cm; 1st Dynasty, Early Dynastic Period; Abydos; Upper Floor, Room 4*
page 273 | ***185. A Girdle of Mereret*** | *JE 30879, JE 30923; gold, amethyst, L. 60cm; 12th Dynasty, Middle Kingdom; Dashur; Upper Floor, Room 4*
pages 276-277 | ***186. A Pendant of Mereret*** | *JE 53070; gold, turquoise, lapis lazuli, carnelian; H. 4.6cm; 12th Dynasty, Middle Kingdom; Dashur; Upper Floor, Room 4*

JE 30879
JE 30923

**CG 52003**

**JE 53070**

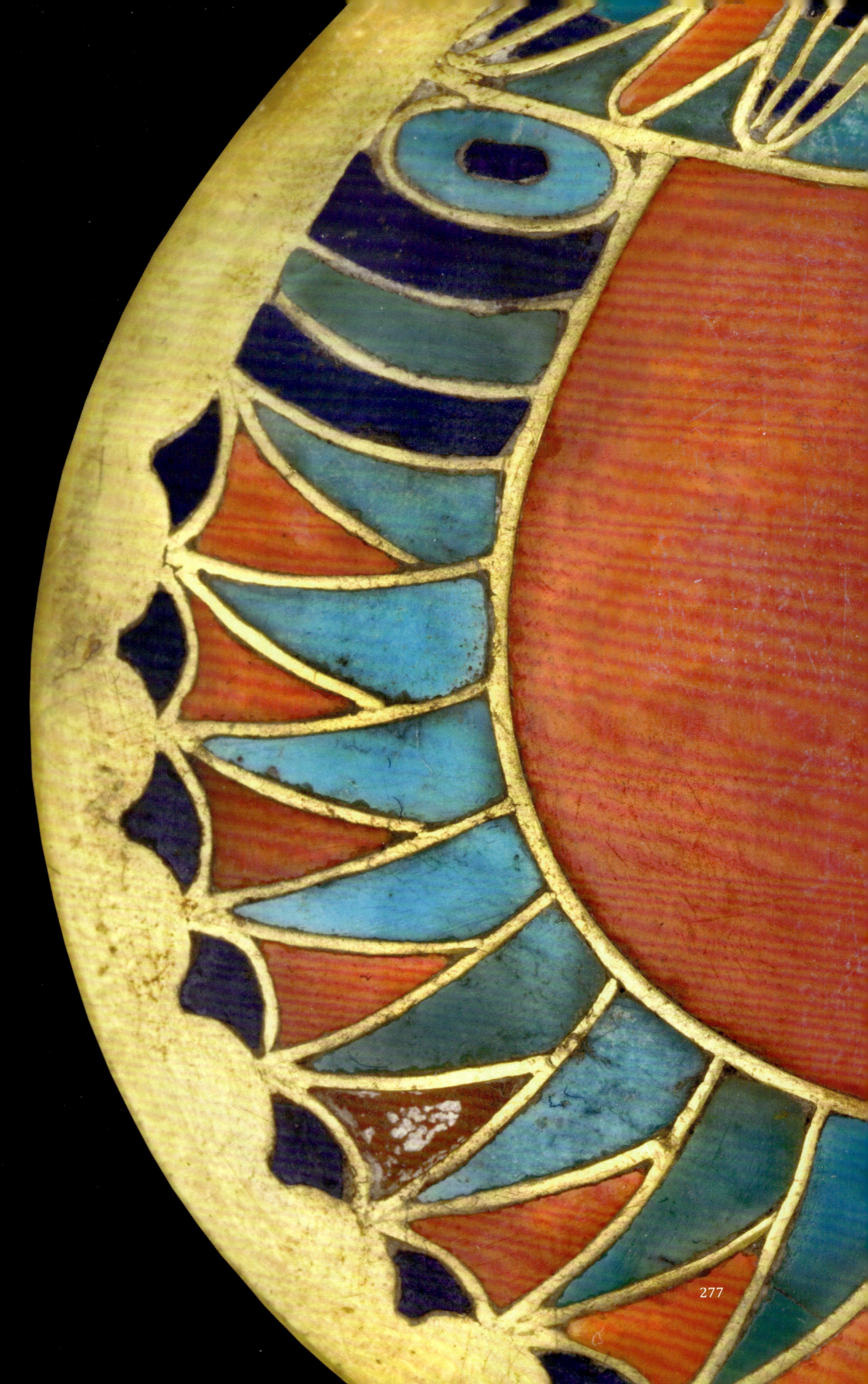

## 187. A Pectoral of Princess Mereret

*CG 52003; gold, carnelian, turquoise, lapis lazuli, amethyst; H. 7.9cm; 12th Dynasty, Middle Kingdom; Dashur; Upper Floor, Room 4*

The main feature of this pectoral is a dual scene of the king, Amenemhat III, smiting enemies. The central hieroglyphs describe him as, the Good God, Lord of the Two Lands and all foreign lands. At the top of the scene the goddess Nekhbet can be seen with her wings outstretched in protection, holding the symbols of life and stability.

## 188. A Pectoral of Sathathor with the Name of Senwosret II

*JE 30857; gold, lapis lazuli, feldspar, carnelian; L. 4.9cm; 12th Dynasty, Middle Kingdom; Dashur; Upper Floor, Room 4*

The frame of this pectoral is topped by a cavetto cornice. Below, at the centre of the piece, is a cartouche of Senwosret II, surmounted by the hieroglyphic symbol for gods. On either side of the cartouche is a hawk, each wearing the Double Crown of Upper and Lower Egypt, and standing on a neb-symbol, meaning gold. Behind each hawk is a cobra and a sun-disc, with each cobra passing through an ankh-symbol. The pectoral is attached to a chain of gold beads, and semiprecious stones.

page 276 | *187. A Pectoral of Princess Mereret* | CG 52003; gold, carnelian, turquoise, lapis lazuli, amethyst; H. 7.9cm; 12th Dynasty, Middle Kingdom; Dashur; Upper Floor, Room 4
page 279 | *188. A Pectoral of Sathathor with the Name of Senwosret II* | JE 30857; gold, lapis lazuli, feldspar, carnelian; L. 4.9cm; 12th Dynasty, Middle Kingdom; Dashur; Upper Floor, Room 4

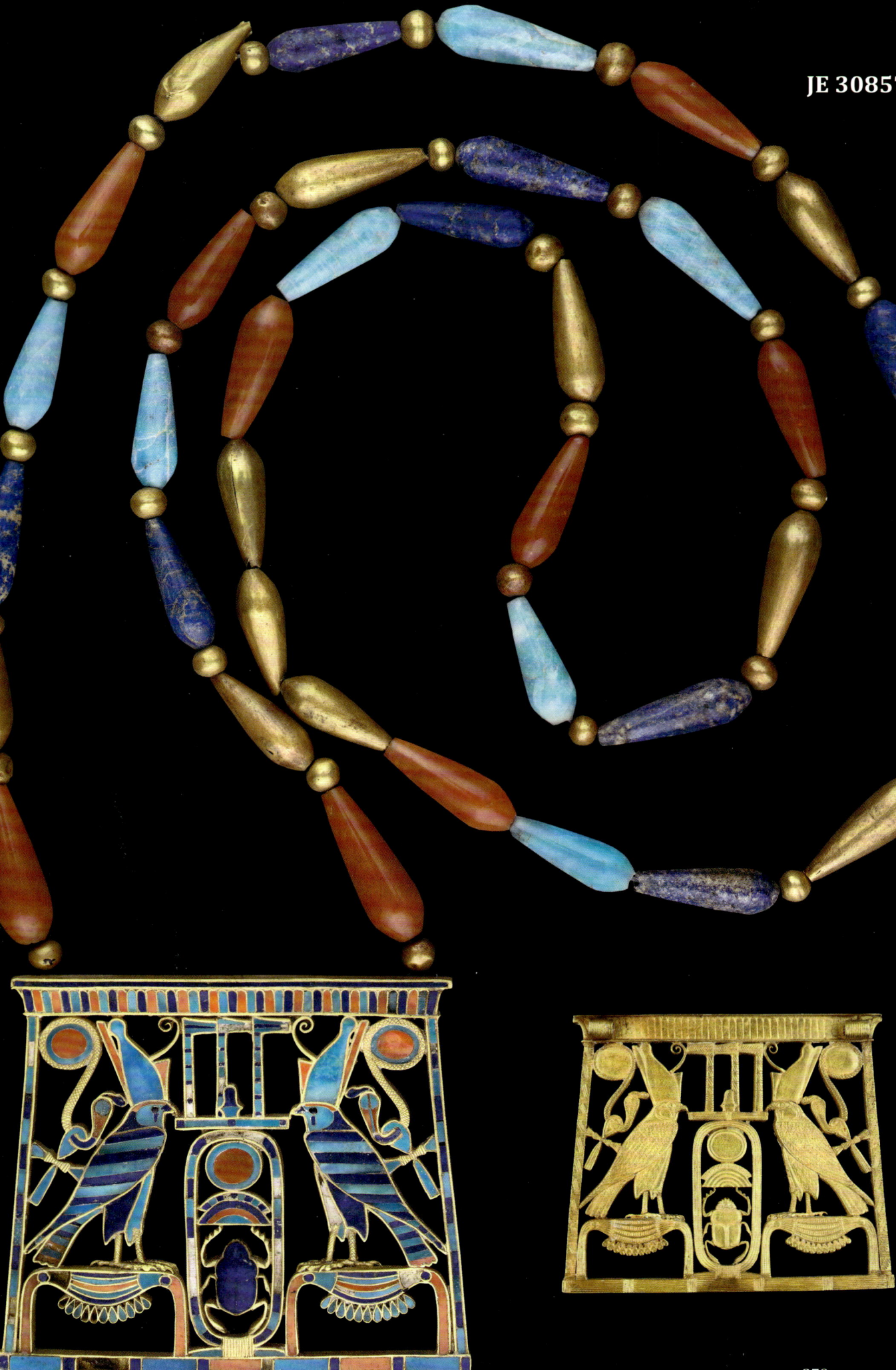

### 189. A Clasp of Princess Sathathor

*JE 30862; gold, lapis lazuli, carnelian, turquoise; 12th Dynasty, Middle Kingdom; Dashur; Upper Floor, Room 4*

This clasp takes the form of two lotus flowers, between them hangs an image of the Goddess Bat. It will originally have fitted to a necklace.

### 190. A Collar of Princess Khnumit

*JE 31113; JE 31115; gold, lapis lazuli, carnelian, turquoise; W. 35cm; 12th Dynasty, Middle Kingdom; Dashur; Upper Floor, Room 4*

This collar ends with two hawk's heads, one green and one blue; these were used to fasten the collar around the neck. Hieroglyphic symbols run along its centre, between two rows of gold beads, representing the words for life, stability, and protection, among others. Small tear-shaped pendants hang from the bottom of the collar. When discovered this collar was in pieces and has since been restored.

### 191. The Diadem of Princess Khnumit

*CG 52860; gold, lapis lazuli, carnelian; D. 64cm; 12th Dynasty, Middle Kingdom; Dashur; Upper Floor, Room 4*

This diadem is composed of two sections; the horizontal part consists of a series of rosettes, connected by flowers, while the vertical section resembles a branch with leaves hanging from it. It is likely that the princess wore this diadem in life during ceremonies.

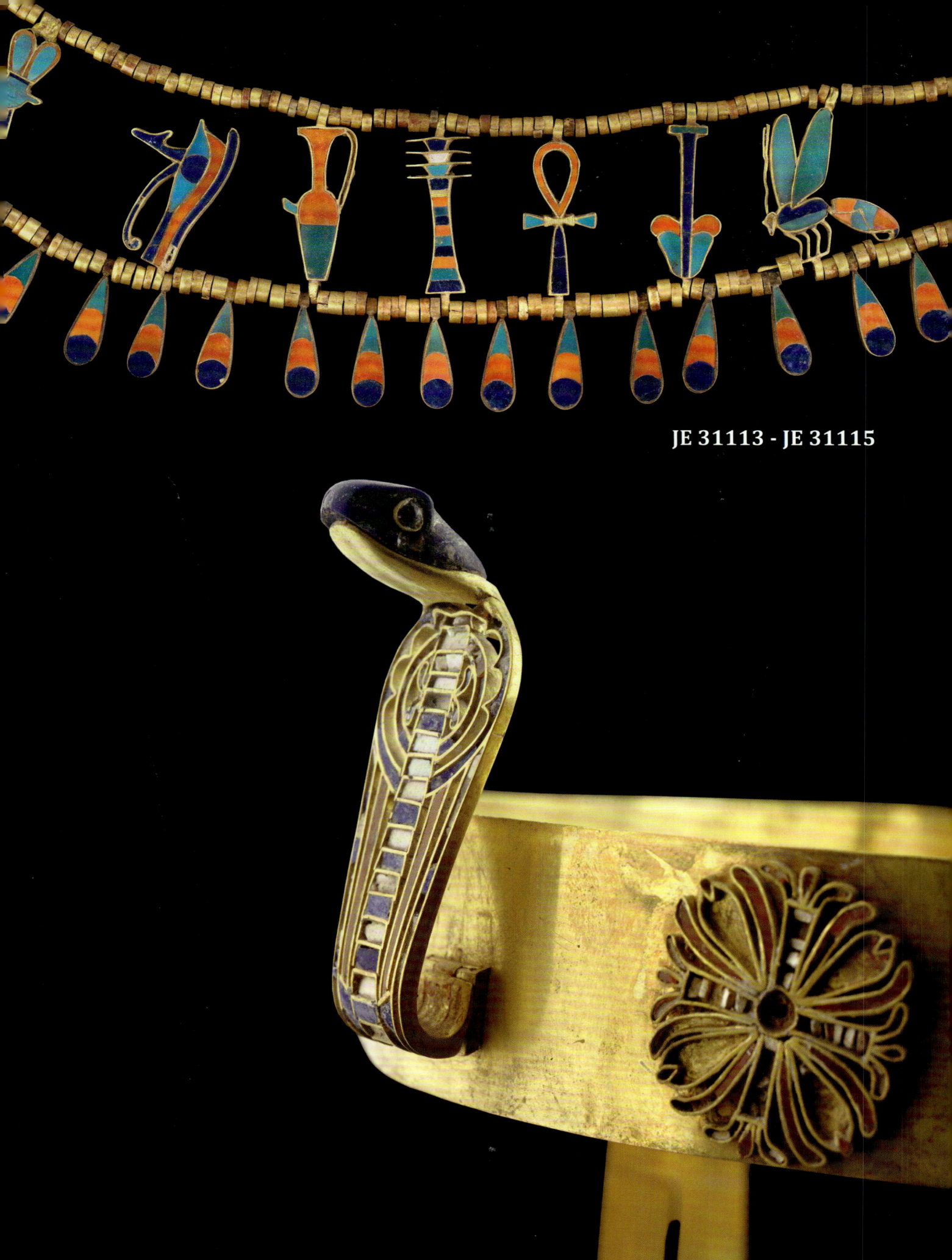

JE 31113 - JE 31115

JE 44919

CG 52860

JE 30862

## 192. The Collar of Princess Neferuptah

*JE 90199; gold, carnelian, feldspar; L. 36.5cm; 12th Dynasty, Middle Kingdom; Hawara, Faiyum; Upper Floor, Room 4*

The Egyptians called this form of collar the *wesekh*, meaning broad. Six rows of beads terminate with the head of a golden falcon at each end; these were used as fasteners. Two smaller chains of beads are attached to the falcons, leading to a counterpoise, which also bears the image of a falcon, with further horizontal rows of beads hanging from it. At the bottom of the collar, teardrop shaped pendants can be seen, connected to a row of small golden beads.

## 193. The Uraeus of Senwosret II

*JE 46694; gold, lapis lazuli, carnelian, feldspar; 12th Dynasty, Middle Kingdom; Lahun; Upper Floor; Room 4*

This uraeus was discovered by Petrie in 1920 during his work around the Pyramid of Senwosret II at Lahun. The rearing cobra, known as a uraeus, was a symbol of royalty, worn at the forehead. This piece was thus likely part of a headdress or crown. It is made from gold with additions of precious stones. It was believed that the uraeus was the Goddess Wadjet of Upper Egypt in the form of a cobra, and that it would spit fire at enemies.

## 194. The Diadem of Princess Sathathor Yunet

*JE 44919; gold, lapis lazuli, carnelian; L. 44cm; 12th Dynasty, Middle Kingdom; Lahun; Upper Floor, Room 4*

The tomb of Sathathor Yunet was found by Petrie near the funerary monuments of Senwosret II at Lahun, in the Faiyum; most of the objects from this tomb are now on display in the Metropolitan Museum of Art, New York. Here we see the princess' diadem; the circular band of gold is decorated with fifteen rosettes and a uraeus at the front. Six bands of gold hang down from the diadem, while two golden feathers rise up at the back. The diadem was made to be worn above the princess' wig.

## 195. The Mirror of Princess Sathathor Yunet

*JE 44920; gold, silver, electrum, semiprecious stones; H. 28cm; 12th Dynasty, Middle Kingdom; Lahun; Upper Floor, Room 4*

This mirror is a masterpiece of Middle Kingdom art. The mirror itself is made from silver, while the handle is of obsidian. The handle takes the form of a papyrus flower, and is also decorated with the face of Hathor.

JE 46694

JE 44920

JE 90199

## 196. The Broad Collar of Queen Ahhotep

*JE 4725a; gold, semiprecious stones; W. 20.80cm; 18th Dynasty, New Kingdom; Dra Abu el-Naga, Luxor; Upper Floor, Room 4*

This collar displays eight rows of decorative features, fixed at each end to a falcon's head. These heads can be connected to one another by a clasp, which allows the collar to be joined around the neck. The decorative features consist of elaborate beads, formed from a modelled front-piece attached to a plain back-piece, through which the string passes. These beads take many different forms: flat metal blade-likes shapes, lions chasing ibexes, cats, winged uraei, vultures, small crosses, bells or lotuses, and coiled cords can all be seen. In total there are 336 pieces.

## 197. The Earrings of Tawosret

*JE 39675; gold; H. 13.5cm; 19th Dynasty, New Kingdom; Valley of the Kings, Luxor; Upper Floor, Room 4*

These earrings, inscribed with the cartouches of Seti II, are each composed of three parts. The lower part presents seven spherical corn-flowers, which hang from a flat central piece bearing royal cartouches. This is attached to the upper part, which consists of a tube and two large circular sections – one a cap, and the other in the form of a rosette. The earrings were found with other objects inscribed for Seti II and Queen Tawosret in the Valley of the Kings.

## 198. The Bracelets of Seti II

*JE 39688a and d; silver; W. 6.5cm; 19th Dynasty, New Kingdom; Valley of the Kings, Luxor; Upper Floor, Room 4*

Two silver bracelets, inscribed for King Seti II, were found among various objects belonging to him and Queen Tawosret in a tomb in the Valley of the Kings. Each shows a scene of Tawosret offering to the enthroned king; she is standing, holding a vase in her left hand, and a flower in the right, while the king holds a cup and a leaf. The names of both can be seen in the cartouches above.

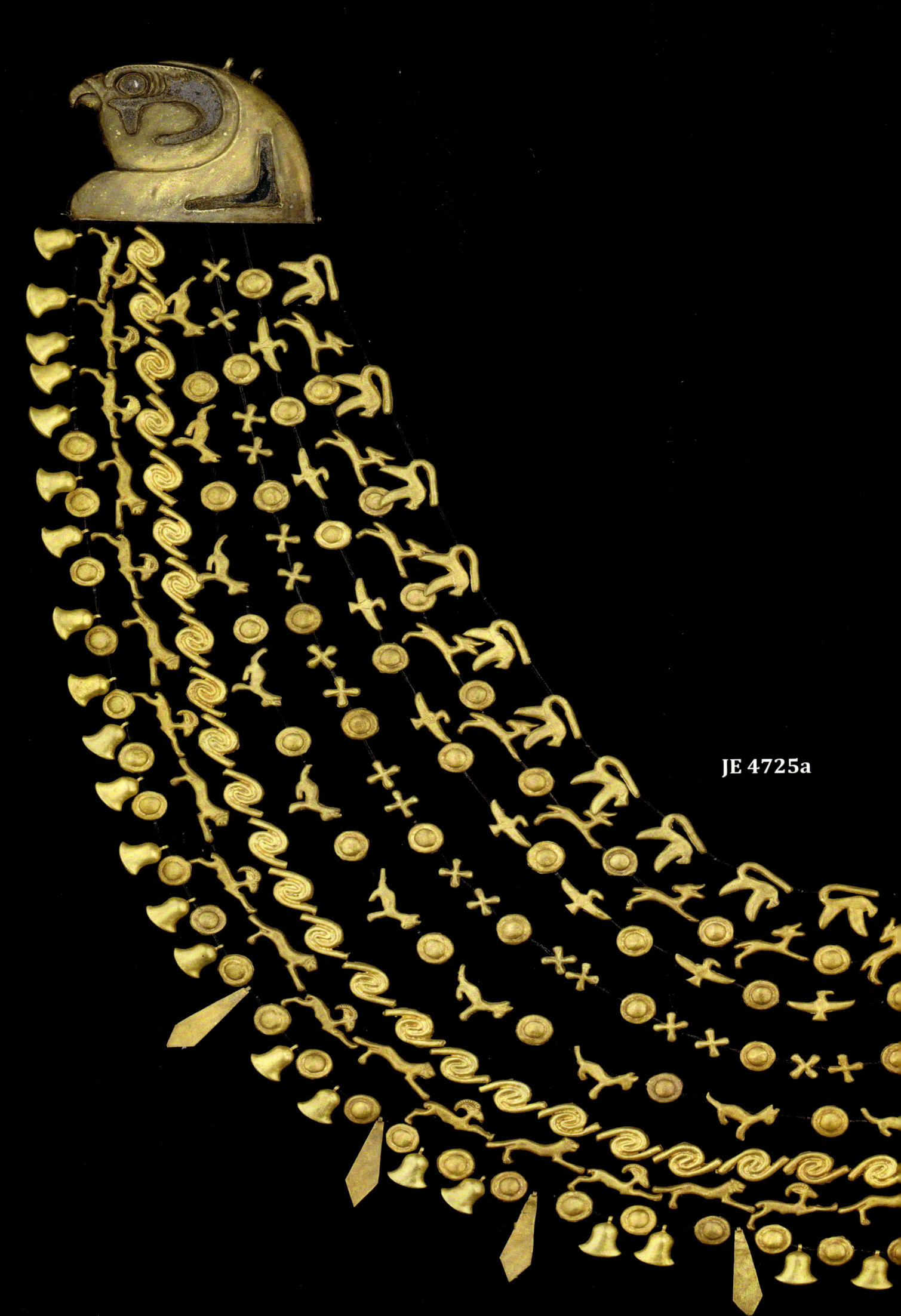

JE 4725a

# The Faiyum Portraits *(Upper Floor, Room 14)*

## A Brief History of the Faiyum Portraits

*From the beginning of Egyptian civilisation the ancient Egyptians believed in resurrection; it was of the utmost importance to spend time in this life preparing for the next. It was especially important for them to protect the body, which they did through mummification. They believed that if the body were to be destroyed the soul would not go to the kingdom of Osiris. As well as preserving the body generally, it was also important to retain the deceased's personal features in a recognisable form so that the soul could find the corpse. In order to achieve this they developed funerary masks, such as the Golden Mask of Tutankhamun. Thus, the Faiyum portraits, although a Roman innovation, developed out of the funerary beliefs of the ancient Egyptians. The paintings can be very vivid and detailed; the faces are shown in a naturalistic manner, showing signs of age, with eyes that seem alive, and the occasional slight smile. We also see the clothes that people wore in their daily lives, and how the fashions changed. The portraits were used in two major ways: many were placed with the mummy at death, while others acted much like modern photographs, with the portrait being hung in the owner's house during life; this is evidenced by portraits existing of the same person at different ages.*

*The portraits reached fame in the 19th century when Theodor Graf, a Venetian antiquities dealer, brought a large number to Europe. They were regarded as so beautiful and realistic that some scholars believed they were fakes, and that a modern artist must have created them. Between 1881 and 1899, the Egyptologist Flinders Petrie, under the supervision of Gaston Maspero, the Director of the Egyptian Museum, conducted excavations in the Faiyum. Petrie discovered two cemeteries of mummies, their faces covered in portraits similar to those already discovered. Petrie found perhaps the most important group of portraits during his excavations in 1888, in the Roman Cemetery at Hawara close to the Pyramid of Amenemhat III; here, he found over 146 beautifully preserved portraits.*

*Although known as the Faiyum Portraits, such objects have been found at many sites across Egypt; from Saqqara in the north to Aswan in the south. Significantly, many paintings, similar in beauty to those of the Faiyum, have been found at Antinoopolis in Middle Egypt - the city that was founded by Emperor Hadrian in 130 AD to the memory of his friend Antonius who drowned in the Nile in this area. The date assigned to each portrait is dependent on a number of stylistic factors, such as the style of the hair or beard, and also the jewellery worn. The earliest examples date to the late 1st century AD, however, the vast majority date to the 2nd and 3rd Centuries AD, with some continuing to be produced in the 4th Century AD. Coins found with the portraits can also help provide dates. The paintings were either made directly onto a wooden panel, sometimes after a layer of plaster had been added, or onto the mummy wrappings. They were made using one of two methods, the tempera method or the encaustic painting method: the tempera method involved mixing pigments together with egg white, while the encaustic method involved the colours being mixed with hot wax.*

*In the future we are planning to build a special museum just for the display of the Faiyum portraits.*

## 199. A Portrait of a Woman

*CG 33243; encaustic painting on wood; H. 42cm; 1st Century AD, Roman Period; Hawara, Faiyum; Upper Floor, Room 14*

This young woman is presented in beautiful colours. We see her from the chest and shoulders up, with her head slightly tilted to her left. She wears a necklace and earrings, indicating that she was a woman of wealth, while her long face has a melancholy expression. Due to her jewellery, this portrait is commonly known as the 'golden young woman.'

page 293 | *199. A Portrait of a Woman* | *CG 33243; encaustic painting on wood; H. 42cm; 1st Century AD, Roman Period; Hawara, Faiyum; Upper Floor, Room 14*

292

293

## 200. A Portrait of a Young Boy

*CG 33260; encaustic painting on wood; H. 35.5cm, end of the 1st Century and beginning of 2nd, Roman Period; Faiyum; Upper Floor, Room 14*

This young boy is presented wearing a golden laurel crown; his face is olive coloured, and the artist has painted his features in wonderful detail; the forehead is lit by a faint light, the mouth is smiling slightly, and the hair is coloured black.

## 201. A Portrait of a Young Woman

*CG 33244; encaustic painting on wood; H. 31cm; 1st Century AD; Roman Period; Faiyum; Upper Floor, Room 14*

The image of this woman is painted on a black background. She has large eyes, with thin eyebrows, and wears expensive earrings and a necklace. Below, she wears a dark purple tunic. It is evident that she was of high standing in society.

## 202. A Portrait of Two Brothers

*CG 33267; encaustic painting on wood; D. 61cm; Antinoopolis; 2nd Century AD, Roman Period; Upper Floor, Room 14*

This portrait is painted on a circular wooden board, and presents two brothers standing side by side. The younger brother, to the left, has light skin and a slight smile. He wears an elaborate tunic, with a cloak held by a clasp. The elder brother, to the right, has darker skin and eyes, with thick lips and a faint moustache. He also wears a white tunic, but it is not as elaborate as that of his brother. Above each brother can be seen a bronze statue of a god. It is likely that the brothers' parents were of different ethnic origins.

296

# V. Bibliography

Aldred C., *Old Kingdom Art in Egypt* (London 1949).

Aldred C., *Middle Kingdom Art in Ancient Egypt* (London, 1950).

Aldred C., *New Kingdom Art in Ancient Egypt during the Eighteenth Dynasty* (London, 1961).

Aldred C., *Jewels of the Pharaohs: Egyptian Jewellery of the Dynastic Period* (London, 1971).

Aldred C., *Akhenaten and Nefertiti* (London & New York, 1973).

Andrews C., *Ancient Egyptian Jewelry* (London, 1990).

Aryton E.R., Currelly C.T., and Weigall A.E., *Abydos*, III (London, 1904).

Baines J. & Malek J., *Atlas of Ancient Egypt* (Oxford, 1980).

Baraize É., 'Compte rendu des travaux exécutés à Déîr-el-Médinéh,' *Annales du Service des Antiquités de l'Égypte 13* (1914), 19-42.

Von Bissing P.F., *Tongefasse, Bis zum Beginn des alten Reiches, Catalogue général des antiquitiés égyptiennes du Musée du Caire*, CG 2001 - 2152 (Vienna, 1913).

Bietak M., 'Zu den nubischen Bogenschützen aus Assiut: ein Beitrag zur Geschichte der Ersten Zwischenzeit,' in *Melanges Gamal Eddin Mokhtar*, I (Cairo, 1985), 87 – 97.

Blackman A.M., *The Rock Tombs of Meir*, I (London, 1914).

Borchardt L., *Statuen und Statuetten von Königen und Privatleuten im Museum zu Kairo, Catalogue général des antiquitiés égyptiennes du Musée du Caire 1 - 1294* (Berlin, 1911 - 1936).

Borchardt L., *Denkmäler des Alten Reiches, Catalogue général des antiquitiés égyptiennes du Musée du Caire 1295 - 1808* (Berlin, 1937 - 1964).

Brunton G., *Lahun, I, The Treasure* (London, 1920).

Bruyère B., *La tombe no 1 de Sen-nedjem à Deir el Médineh* (Cairo, 1959).

Carter H., 'Report on the Tomb of Mentuhotep Ist at Deir el-Bahari, Known as Bab el-Hocan,' *Annales du Service des Antiquités de l'Égypte 2* (1901), 201 – 205.

Carter H. (with Mace A.C.), *The Tomb of Tut.ankh.Amen*, 3 vols (London, 1923 – 1933).

Cherpion N., 'De quand date la tombe du nain Seneb?,' *Bulletin de l'Institut Français d'Archéologie Orientale 84 (1984)*, 35-54 (fig., pl.).

Daressy G., *Fouilles de la Vallée des Rois <1898-1899>, Catalogue général des antiquités égyptiennes du Musée du Caire 24009 – 24990* (Cairo, 1902).

Daressy G., *Statues des divinités, Catalogue général des antiquités égyptiennes du Musée du Caire 38001 - 39348* (Cairo, 1905 - 1906).

Davis Th., *The Tomb of Iouiya and Touiyou* (London, 1907).

Davis Th., *The Tomb of Queen Tiyi, Catalogue of the Objects Discovered* (London, 1910).

Davies N.M., & Gardiner A.H., *Tutankhamun's Painted Box* (Oxford, 1962).

Desroches-Noblecourt Ch., *L'art égyptien* (Paris, 1962).

Desroches-Noblecourt Ch., *Tutankhamen, Life and Death of a Pharaoh* (New York, 1963).

Eaton-Krauss M., 'Miscellanea Amarnensia,' *Chronique d'Égypte 56* (1981), 245-264.

Farag N. and Iskander Z., *The Discovery of Neferwptah* (Cairo, 1971).

Gaballa G. A., *Narrative in Egyptian Art* (Mainz, 1976).

Gardiner A.H., Peet T.E., and Černý J., *The Inscriptions of Sinai, II* (London, 1955).

Ghalioungui P., 'Sur l'exophthalmie de quelques statuettes de l'Ancien Empire,' *Bulletin de l'Institut Français d'Archéologie Orientale 62* (1964), 63-65 (4 pl.).

Habachi L., 'The So-Called Hyksos Monuments Reconsidered. Apropos of the Discovery of a Dyad of Sphinxes,' *Studien zur altägyptischen Kultur 6* (1978), 79-92.

Hawass Z., 'Unique Statues from Giza V, The Exceptional Statue of the Priest Kai and his Family,' in Daoud K., Bedier S., & Abd el-Fatah S. (eds) *Studies in Honor of Ali Radwan*, II (Cairo, 2005), 25-38.

Hawass Z., 'A Group of Unique Statues Discovered at Giza. III: The Statues of inty-Sdw from Tomb GSE 1915,' in Grimal N. (ed.) *Les critères de datation stylistiques* (Cairo, 1998), 187-208.

Hawass Z., 'A Group of Unique Statues Discovered at Giza. II: An Unfinished Reserve Head and a Statuette of an Overseer,' in *Kunst des Alten Reiches. Symposium im Deutschen Archäologischen Institut Kairo am 29. und 30. Oktober 1991* (Mainz, 1995), 97 – 101.

Hawass Z., 'The Statue of the Dwarf Pr-n(j)-anx(w) Recently Discovered at Giza,' *Mitteilungen des Deutschen Archäologischen Instituts Kairo 47* (1991), 157-162.

Hawass Z., 'The Khufu Statuette: is it an Old Kingdom Sculpture?,' in Posener-Kriéger P. (ed.) *Melanges Gamal Eddin Mokhtar, I*, (Cairo, 1985), 379-394.

Jones D., *Model Boats from the Tomb of Tutankhamun* (Oxford, 1990).

Lacau P., *Stèles du Nouvel Empire, Catalogue général des antiquitiés égyptiennes du Musée du Caire 34001 - 34068* (Cairo, 1909 - 1926).

Lacau P., *Stèles de la XVIII. Dyn., Catalogue général des antiquitiés égyptiennes du Musée du Caire 34087 - 34189* (Cairo, 1957).

Leclant J., *Montouemhat, quatrième prophète d'Amon, Prince de la ville* (Le Caire, 1961).

Lefèbvre G., *Le tombeau de Petosiris*, 3 vols (Cairo, 1923-1924).

Legrain G., *Statues et statuettes de rois et de particuliers, Catalogue général des antiquitiés égyptiennes du Musée du*

298

*Caire 42001 – 42250* (Cairo, 1906-1925).

Lehner M., *The Pyramid Tomb of Hetep-heres and the Satellite Pyramid of Khufu* (Mainz, 1985).

Martin G., 'Notes on a Canopic Jar from Kings' Valley Tomb 55,' *Mélanges Gamal Eddin Mokhtar, II* (Cairo, 1985), 111 – 124.

Al-Masri Y., 'Preliminary Report on the Excavations in Akhmim by the Egyptian Antiquities Organization,' *Annales du Service des Antiquités de l'Égypte 69* (1983), 7-13.

Montet P., 'Inscriptions de Basse Époque trouvées à Tanis,' *Kêmi* 8 (1946), 29-126.

Montet P. , *Psousennès, La nécropole royale de Tanis,* II, (Paris, 1951).

De Morgan J., *Fouilles a Dahchour en 1894 - 1895* (Vienna, 1903).

Millet N. B., 'The Reserve Heads of the Old Kingdom,' in Simpson W. K. & Davis W. M. (eds) *Studies in Ancient Egypt, the Aegean, and the Sudan. Essays in honor of Dows Dunham on the occasion of his 90th birthday,* June 1, 1980 (Boston, 1981), 122–131.

Murray M., & Nuttall M., *A Handlist to Howard Carter's Catalogue of Objects in Tutankhamun's Tomb* (Oxford, 1963).

Naville E., *The XIth Dynasty Temple at Deir el-Bahari,* 3 vols (London, 1907 - 1913).

Petrie W.M.F., *Meidum* (London, 1892).

Petrie W. M. F., *Six Temples at Thebes* (London, 1897).

Petrie W.M.F., *The Royal Tombs of the Earliest Dynasties,* II (London 1901).

Petrie W.M.F., *Researches in Sinai* (London, 1906).

Petrie W.M.F., Brunton G., & Murray M. A., *Lahun, II* (London, 1923).

Piankoff A., *The Shrines of Tut-Ankh-Amon* (New York, 1955).

Porter B. & Moss R. L. B., *Topographical Bibliography of Ancient Egyptian Hieroglyphic Texts, Reliefs, and Paintings, 2nd Ed. with Burney E. W. & Málek J.;* 7 vols (Oxford, 1927 – 1952; 2nd ed. 1960).

Quibell J.E., *Archaic Objects, Catalogue général des antiquités égyptiennes du Musée du Caire 11001 - 12000* (Cairo, 1904 – 1905).

Quibell J.E., *Hierakonpolis,* I (London, 1900).

Quibell J.E. & Green F.W., *Hierakonpolis,* II (London, 1902).

Quibell J.E., *The Tomb of Yuaa and Thuiu, Catalogue général des antiquités égyptiennes du Musée du Caire 51001 - 51191* (Cairo, 1908).

Quibell J.E., *Excavations at Saqqara (1911-12), the Tomb of Hesy* (Cairo, 1913).

Ranke H., *Masterpieces of Egyptian Art* (London, 1951).

Reisner G. A., Mycerinus, *The Temples of the Third Pyramid at Giza* (Cambridge, Massachusetts, 1931).

Reisner G. A. & Smith W. S., *A History of the Giza Necropolis, II* (Cambridge, Massachusetts, 1955).

Riefstahl E., *Patterned Textiles in Pharaonic Egypt* (Brooklyn, 1944).

Russmann E. R., *The Representation of the King in the XXVth Dynasty* (Brussels & Brooklyn, 1974).

Saad Z. Y., 'A Preliminary Report on the Excavations at Saqqara 1939-1940,' *Annales du Service des Antiquités de l'Égypte 40* (1940) 675-693.

Saleh M. & Sourouzian H., *The Egyptian Museum Cairo Official Catalogue* (Cairo, 1987).

Smith G.E., *The Royal Mummies, Catalogue général des antiquités égyptiennes du Musée du Caire 61051 – 61100* (Cairo, 1912).

Smith W. S., *The Art and Architecture of Ancient Egypt,* revised by Simpson W. K. (New Haven & London, 1998).

Stadelmann R., *Die Ägyptischen Pyramiden* (Mainz, 1985).

Stadelmann R., 'Ramses II., Harmachis und Hauron,' *in J. Osing & G. Dreyer (eds) Form und Mass. Beiträge zur Literatur, Sprache und Kunst des alten Ägypten. Festschrift für Gerhard Fecht zum 65. Geburtstag am 6. Februar 1987* (Wiesbaden, 1987), 436–449.

Touny A.D. & Wenig S., *Der Sport im Alten Agypten* (Leipzig, 1969).

Vandersleyen Cl., 'La Date du Cheikh el-Beled,' *Journal of Egyptian Archaeology 69* (1983), 61–65.

Vandier J., *Manuel d'archéologie Égyptienne,* 6 vols (Paris, 1952–1978).

Varille A., *Inscription concernant l'architecte Amehotep fils de Hapou* (Cairo, 1968).

Verner M., 'Statue of Twēret (Cairo Museum no. 39145) Dedicated by Pabēsi and Several Remarks on the Role of the Hippopotamus Goddess,' *Zeitschrift für ägyptische Sprache und Altertumskunde 96,* 1 (1969), 52-63.

Verner M., 'Les sculptures de Rêneferef découvertes à Abousir,' *Bulletin de l'Institut Français d'Archéologie Orientale*

Vernier É., *Bijoux et orfèvreries, Catalogue général des antiquités égyptiennes du Musée du Caire 52001 - 53855* (Cairo, 1927).

Wildung D., *Sesostris und Amenemhet, Ägypten im Mittleren Reich* (Munich, 1984).

Winlock H.E., *Excavations at Deir el-Bahari* (New York, 1942).

Winlock H.E., *Models of Daily Life in Ancient Egypt* (New York, 1955).

Woods W., 'A Reconstruction of the Triads of King Mycerinus,' *Journal of Egyptian Archaeology 60* (1974), 82–93.

Yoyotte J., *Treasures of the Pharaohs* (Geneva, 1968).